CW01432774

ADHD

HOW GREAT MINDS TURN ADHD TO THEIR ADVANTAGE

KAMALA PARK

Copyright © 2018
All rights reserved.
ISBN: 1984171119
ISBN-13: 978-1984171115

TABLE OF CONTENTS

1 ADHD IS A GIFT

ADHD is a gift! Don't believe me? Well, why would you when the majority of the dialogue and terminology surrounding ADHD suggests otherwise? The truth is, we've been conditioned to believe it's a "disorder," something "out of order," and therefore wrong. But if there's anything this century has taught us, it is to embrace diversity, and not to criticize or vilify difference. What happens then when we take a different approach to ADHD and, instead of considering it a disadvantage, we focus on the benefits inherent in having attention deficit hyperactivity disorder (there's that frustrating word again)?

Neither I nor either of my children have been diagnosed with ADHD, but my experience of working directly with children and adults who "suffer" (ugh) from the condition compelled me to research the topic further. The consequence of this was the overwhelming epiphany that the preconceptions surrounding the condition need to change because there are many attributes of ADHD worth exploiting for the benefit of the individual diagnosed as well as their family, friends, and co-workers.

This is not to say that those diagnosed do not actually suffer. Evidence shows that ADHD can have a negative effect on a variety of emotional and cognitive levels. Many but not all of those with ADHD can experience low self-esteem, become disengaged with the education system and struggle to understand and interpret their symptoms. Experiencing any of this can be incredibly frustrating and ostracizing. Behavioral therapies and stimulant medications are the most common medically-backed treatments to help reduce hyperactivity, inattention, and impulsiveness. Non-stimulant medications can also be prescribed, and in some cases, doctors may recommend antidepressants. Whilst the Food and Drug Administration is yet to approve the use of such medications to treat ADHD, it is clear that they may be of benefit to those dealing with the social and personal difficulties arising from the relatively common ADHD by-product of low self-esteem.

However, I would like to challenge the common use of the terms "suffer," "suffering from," and "sufferer" in relation to ADHD. Along with the misnomer "disorder," it is assumed that the symptoms of ADHD are purely negative in their impact, while the advantages that can be drawn from symptoms such as hyperactivity are not taken into account.

I'm not trying to start a revolution. I'm not suggesting that those with ADHD have a secret super power that is unattainable for the rest of us.

Neither am I claiming that there isn't any positive dialogue out there – there definitely is. You just have to look a little harder for it.

What I am claiming is that there are abundant reasons why those with ADHD (and their parents, carers, teachers, friends, and co-workers) should not consider the diagnosis a "disadvantage." Instead, this guide should serve to encourage everyone to explore their full potential, free from the shackles of negative perception.

That does not mean the scientists and doctors are wrong; it just means that our interpretation of their advice need not be so negative. I am not suggesting that getting a diagnosis is like winning the personality lottery, but when understood and managed the right way, ADHD can present certain advantages to the individual. My hope is that by combining medical advice with learning to tap into the gifts ADHD encompasses, our collective mindset and consequent actions and attitudes can change so that no one feels disadvantaged because of a diagnosis.

Try to think of it as a game – a good one, with huge rewards at the end. You've been dealt the cards, and it's now up to you how to play them. Use this guide to help you recognize that winning at life can be easy once you play the ADHD advantage.

Unwrapping your Potential

Still don't believe me? How about listening to some of these people – you'll never guess what they all have in common...

Justin Timberlake – Grammy-winning artist

Jamie Oliver – Celebrity chef and food activist

Karina Smirnoff – *Dancing With the Stars* pro

Will Smith – Actor and singer

Michael Phelps – Olympic gold-medalist for swimming

Joan Rivers – Comedian, actress, writer, producer, host

Sir Richard Branson – Virgin Group owner and adventurer

Terry Bradshaw – Former NFL quarterback

James Carville – Political consultant and

commentator

Emma Watson – Actress and United Nations Ambassador

Ty Pennington – *Extreme Makeover: Home Edition* host

Jim Carrey, Bruce Jenner, Zooey Deschanel…The list could go on for pages and pages, but you get the idea. The point is, all of these hugely successful people have spoken publicly about their ADHD diagnosis – and some received a very late diagnosis – and yet, they all have pursued highly competitive vocations, each achieving distinction and acclaim for their respective endeavors.

My point is simple. Just because you have ADHD, it does *not* mean you lack in potential. In fact, I hope you will come to realize that your potential is one of the things that set you apart; you just have to learn to see it for what it is and nurture it to fruition.

Each chapter within this guide addresses a distinct characteristic common within those diagnosed with ADHD. You may recognize a few instantly and come to the conclusion that many of these attributes are found in those you know who have ADHD – whether that be yourself or someone in your family or social circle.

All of these characteristics harbor the potential for greatness if directed effectively, which is exactly what some of the famous names above have done. Through a process of self-assessment, self-enlightenment, and self-acceptance, these gifts can become powerful weapons to conquer a world that might have become hostile and difficult to understand.

With each characteristic, we'll challenge the negative assumptions that it may garner, and – more importantly – we'll learn how to turn each of them to our advantage. Alongside this, we'll reflect on the various complementary therapies and toys that should work comfortably in conjunction with any of your doctor's recommendations.

An excellent example of this attitude of challenge is the transformation experienced by my neighbor's son (and consequently my neighbor) after I taught him some mindfulness techniques to control his ADHD symptoms. He had become used to banging his head and limbs in frustration when he felt out of control and confused. After just a few weeks of mindfulness coaching, his self-abuse diminished – it almost disappeared entirely – and was replaced with mindfulness exercises, which he learnt to choose over the banging. It was a win-win situation. He got control over his symptoms as well as some inner quiet; his mother became calmer and less fraught because she no longer needed to fight him to stop the physical behavior detrimental to his health, and consequently, he stopped associating his symptoms and related behavior with a negative reaction from his mother. Plus, I received numerous baked goods which were sent to me in gratitude. So a win-win-win, really!

Potential is something we all begin our lives with an abundance of. Something as simple as a diagnosis can easily destroy this by creating self-doubt and even, as my neighbor's boy was presenting, self-loathing. But it doesn't have to. Take inspiration from the many success stories of the ADHD-advantaged, and begin to unwrap your own, individual gift.

Understanding the Package

Once you begin to peel back the layers of preconception and look more closely at your own diagnosis and what it means to you as an individual, the world around you starts to change. Even more strikingly, your understanding of yourself begins to change, and you may find yourself defining your personality and character under new terms. ADHD, as any condition, comes in a number of forms. Most simply put, these are: predominantly inattentive type (where you are easily distracted, but don't struggle with hyperactivity or impulsiveness), predominantly hyperactive/impulsive type (with no real issue focusing, but rather the need to focus on multiple tasks at once and to flit from one to the next without hesitation or thought), and combined type (a mix of all the major ADHD symptoms). Of course, what we have to remember is that these symptoms can manifest themselves differently in everyone.

Knowing your own strengths and weaknesses is crucial to managing your condition successfully and making it work for you. The above "types" are simply umbrella terms used to describe a range of symptoms that can display themselves in many ways. Considering these symptoms in terms of their potential rather than the limitations and obstacles they might impose can be a challenge when we've been brainwashed by a common ideology to think negatively about ADHD, but once your mindset shifts, the possibilities are endless.

Celebrity chef and campaigner Jamie Oliver has

successfully used nutrition and healthy eating as a way of managing his ADHD symptoms. Olympic athlete Bruce Jenner recognizes now, with the benefit of hindsight, that being the fastest sprinter in his class gave him a positive direction for both his energy and focus. Paul Orfalea, the founder of Kinko's, credits his ADHD with giving him the curiosity to see if he could accomplish his goals. There are as many positive associations with ADHD as there are successful people diagnosed with the condition.

Of course, it's far easier to see the positive when you're in the privileged position of already having accomplished great things. What I hope to do here is to open your mind to your full potential in order to inspire you to go on and achieve your goals. It's important to remember that not all goals involve becoming world-famous! Whether you're eager to publish your own novel, climb the management ladder at work, or simply learn to manage your symptoms, the following chapters are all about how ADHD can provide you with the tools you need to achieve this.

As we go on to explore some of the more common traits apparent in ADHD success stories, take the time to consider which characteristics apply to you, your child, or your loved one personally. These are the keys to unlocking the full potential of the gift.

2 BEING A VISIONARY

Being a visionary does not mean having hallucinations or being able to predict the future. But it's close! Those diagnosed with ADHD are recognized as having the skill to see beyond the present, meaning that they can envision a different future, a different outcome, or a different path towards a goal. They have greater capability to visualize potential solutions or future possibilities, while the rest of us sometimes struggle to see outside the box we're locked in. This creative and indirect approach to problem-solving is often referred to as "lateral thinking." Most of us follow common logical pathways in order to solve a problem, but lateral thinkers are comfortable throwing logic out of the window and have the capacity to approach several potential solutions from various angles.

I'm not afraid to admit that, personally, I'm a fan of logic. It makes sense to me, and I trust the stepping-stone process of following a vertical path to a single solution. But I do sometimes wish that I had the ability to think differently. Companies often seek to employ lateral thinkers because they feel it gives them an edge – it allows them to innovate and expand their brand's potential. And, of course, they are right.

Simply put, lateral thinking is approaching a problem from a different angle, and accepting that there may be more than one solution to it.

For example, imagine you are lost in an unfamiliar wilderness and come across a vast lake. On the other side of the lake, you can make out signs of civilization, but you cannot swim. Logical thinkers are likely to do one of two things: either search for a route around the lake or search for means of constructing something which can carry them across the lake. Both solutions here could be effective but are incredibly time-consuming and also fraught with possible further hazards. With no knowledge of the lake, it could take days or weeks to walk around it, and there may be dangers lying within its depths that make an attempted raft crossing precarious at best. (If it were down to me to build the raft, then "precarious" would be a significant understatement.)

Someone with the capacity for lateral thinking, however, is likely to approach the problem differently. Instead of looking for a way to get themselves across the lake to civilization, they might recognize the opportunity to signal for help, perhaps by creating a fire and a smoke signal, so that the people on the other side of the lake, who presumably have knowledge of its potential dangers, can come and rescue them. It seems obvious and incredibly clever once you've heard it, but the chances of me thinking of that with my logic-centered brain are non-existent. Hence the ADHD advantage.

ADHDers who tap into their lateral thinking skills can therefore be a true asset – and not just when lost in the wilderness. Invite one or two to a brainstorming meeting and watch them wow the crowd with their constant idea generation and dynamic perspective on the issue. A person with ADHD is rarely satisfied with just one answer to a question – they'll give you ten, and continue to look for potential solutions until asked to stop and focus their energy on just one or two. Any CEO who can't see this ability as an asset is missing out on an incredible opportunity.

The capability of seeing the world and consequently interpreting it differently can give you a huge advantage. The trick lies in helping others to understand how your perspective is beneficial to them, without them perceiving it as a threat.

A Kaleidoscope View

Perspective is everything. When I was a child, I used to have a recurrent nightmare where I found myself falling through the blackness of a kaleidoscope as it changed patterns. I have no idea why this was frightening to me, but it definitely was at the time.

ADHD visionaries are less likely to be so perturbed by a simple dream for the reason that they feel great comfort from recognizing the changing patterns in the world. Because they are also extremely competent at finding patterns in chaos, they can see the potential in the little colored beads to reshape into varied, equally beautiful transformations of their previous forms.

It is hard to understand how such a positive quality can have any negative connotations, but we're used to hearing that ADHDers need order and routine, and that consequently they can't cope well with the chaos of irregular situations or environments. This, in turn, suggests that they cannot adapt to difficult or unusual circumstances. Whilst some ADHDers may indeed struggle with this early on in life (or before diagnosis and consequent self-enlightenment), once they learn of their ability to find patterns in chaos and how to use it to make sense of the new environment, they can easily adapt to any scenario. So much so that they are capable of being innovators at times when most are still trying to see the wood for the trees. The skilled ADHDer will use their need for patterns and order to make sense out of disarray, and can then, like a kaleidoscope, show the rest of the world the beauty of the situation. If the world struggles to understand this potential initially, the ADHDer has a remarkable ability to reshape the idea into another form again and again, until the rest of the community is smiling with him or her. Shapeshifters or kaleidoscopes – call them what you will – they possess a remarkable talent that can open up the eyes of others to the many potential outcomes of a state of affairs. Focus on the positive ones, and you'll prove yourself invaluable.

Once an ADHDer has mastered this ability and is using their power for good, there's a risk that they'll feel they are the only person capable of seeing the right solutions. This can make others wary of such approach and advice. Be conscious that although your lateral thinking, idea-generating ability, and propensity to find order in chaos are excellent skills, they are not the only successful tools in approaching a problem. Logic has its merits too. Whilst chances are an ADHDer is likely to find a viable solution faster than others (because he is processing so many potential solutions at once and considering the problem from many different angles at the same time), that doesn't mean other options aren't worth considering too.

If you find yourself in this situation, remain

assertive but not aggressive while putting your ideas forward. Practice "active listening" in order to understand the ideas of others; this gives you the advantage of being able to contribute to their ideas too, and collaborative solutions are often most beneficial to everyone.

Active Listening

Active listening is an art that most people would benefit from learning, but it can be particularly difficult for predominantly inattentive types to learn because of the single-minded focus it requires. Most of us are pretty bad at active listening; we listen, get the gist of what the other person is saying, nod, and make backchanneling interjections to suggest we are following. These are important communication features to encourage the speaker, but too often we are simply "going through the motions" of listening, and our minds may well be elsewhere. Research suggests that we only actually retain 25-50% of what someone says to us, and this percentage will reduce even further for predominantly inattentive ADHD types. The purpose of active listening is to increase this percentage so that we become better at working together, more empathetic and understanding, and we can improve our own efficiency because we've understood what is required of us.

Active listening is all about trying to make sure you are fully "in the moment" and engaged in the conversation you are having. Here are some tips you can practice in order to become a better active listener:

Do

- Concentrate on the speaker's physical communication signals as well as their words (are they defensively crossing their arms, or are they so excited about the topic that they are gesticulating wildly?)
- Try to make eye contact with the speaker to show you are engaged
- Repeat important words or phrases back to the speaker to show you have understood
- Summarize and paraphrase where necessary in order to confirm understanding
- Keep an open mind
- Ask appropriate questions

Don't

- Interrupt unnecessarily
- Get drawn into side conversations or tangents
- Start forming objections or judgments in your mind

If you find it particularly difficult to prevent your mind from wandering, a simple trick to stay focused is to repeat the speaker's words in your mind as they say them. Try doing this regularly for short periods of time to begin with. Active listening is a skill you can train yourself to use. You'll find the benefits are almost instant: improved communication skills, enriched relationships with friends, family, and colleagues, and greater productivity.

Of course, it's important to still feel like your own ideas are valid, and if you're excited about them, then chances are others will be too. Just remember to keep an open mind and to value how others may be able to contribute to the final vision.

The Potential in Patterns

Being an ideas generator is an incredible bonus and a skill that comes to many ADHDers naturally. However, training yourself to deal with unusual situations and to find patterns that make you feel more secure and confident may be a little trickier. The good news is, once you've got the hang of it, this will soon become natural to you too.

A key study published by The University of Western Australia in 2006 identified a cyclical routine for ADHDers trying to make order from chaos. The research suggested that adults with ADHD live in a state of chaos, then strive to control it, achieve control temporarily, and ultimately lose it again, finding themselves back at the original chaotic starting point.

It sounds exhausting, but I think it's worth focusing on the principal findings with regard to the states of being in control and losing control. Simply being cognizant of the contributing factors for finding control and losing it again gives you a huge advantage when trying to both achieve control and maintain it. The very process of striving for control, finding it, losing it, and repeating the cycle already makes an ADHDer quite the expert in being able to find order where it seems there is none – but I think we can agree that being able to maintain order and control is preferable all-around.

It is when you're comfortably in a state of control that it becomes possible to find patterns that can benefit yourself and others. Let's start with the basics:

Five factors that help ADHDers to feel in control

1. Education. This begins, of course, with a diagnosis and with knowing what you have to educate yourself in. ADHD is a complex condition with several differing presentations, so knowing your own type of ADHD as well as how it typically manifests itself within you is vital. Once you understand and acknowledge that there is a reason behind your behavior and personality traits, self-acceptance can quickly replace self-despair and self-loathing. This is obviously much easier to achieve as an adult than as a child, but there are ways of helping children too. Accepting a diagnosis and then actively educating yourself about ADHD is hugely empowering. You're already on course for self-empowerment if you're reading this book – well done you! – but there's plenty out there you can access to help you understand your personal ADHD symptoms. Seek out the knowledge and become an expert in *you*.

2. Sharing the experience. Great comfort comes from realizing you are not alone in your struggle. Knowing that others experience the same difficulties and frustrations, and that they have encountered the same barriers and hurdles, not only opens your mind to self-acceptance, but it also provides you with a wealth of resources. Learning how others manage their symptoms is all part of your education. Unburdening yourself of the anger and fears you may have been bottling up is also a cathartic process which allows for greater

control of your mind. Search for ADHD support groups in your area or try some online forums. There's a fantastic network of fellow ADHDers out there who have embraced their condition, are thriving, and would love to help you to do the same.

3. Medication. This one is a bit of a no-brainer. Tried and tested stimulant prescriptions, along with a variety of alternatives (including complementary therapies), are regularly and successfully used to "tame" the symptoms of ADHD. Those on stimulant drugs claim they feel a greater sense of control and can focus better as well as for significantly longer periods of time. Listening to the advice of medical practitioners and following a medical care plan could substantially increase your ability to maintain control.

4. The significant other. This factor should not be underestimated. ADHDers report that they feel far more capable of maintaining control when they have someone close to them they can rely on for support. This could be a spouse or romantic partner, a friend, a mentor, a medical professional, or someone from a support group. Having someone who understands you and can support you through times of difficulty is important to us all, but can make an exceptional difference to those with ADHD. Removing that feeling of isolation and the feeling that "nobody gets it" also removes the potential self-doubt and self-loathing that so easily occur when symptoms flare up. It may be difficult at first, but be prepared to open

up to someone and trust them with your insecurities. Having a person you can rely on in this way helps you to feel less vulnerable, rather than more so.

5. Job satisfaction. Leading the way vocationally is one way ADHDers feel more secure. Commonly, this means working for themselves, but it can also be as simple as recognizing successes in the workplace, however minor. Having a rewarding career and a sense of job satisfaction are obvious ways to feel valued and successful, and both reassert a sense of you being in control and capable. If you find yourself unhappy with work or feeling undervalued, brainstorm or list all the things you have achieved in your chosen occupation. Write down everything from training course certificates to degrees and PhDs, from a recent "thank you" from a customer to a commendation or promotion. Allowing yourself to take responsibility for any workplace success nurtures your self-worth and reinforces your sense of control.

Five factors that contribute to ADHDers losing control

1. Disillusionment with medical treatment. Medication can feel like a magic wand – a quick fix solution to your difficulties – but treatments vary, and people vary, which means that finding the right medication for you might take some time along with trial and error. Naturally, , you may lose a little faith. Patience is not a strong point in ADHDers, but perseverance is, and there's a very

fine line between the two. Instead of seeing the process a series of failed attempts, try to look at it as a journey towards an ultimate goal with some obstacles along the way. If "wellness" is your ultimate destination, you can consider the treatment process as the path required to get there: sometimes hazardous, sometimes with mirages of false hope, but a path worth persevering on with determination. If you are a significant other to someone diagnosed with ADHD, then these diversions and obstacles are times when you can really help.

2. Frustration over the time lost. There's an inherent irony with this one. Whilst it's only natural to be miffed about the years you went undiagnosed and misunderstood, letting this frustration impair your present to the extent that you are once again out of control and back to square one would be a mournful misdirection of energy. Instead, train your mind to be grateful for the time that's been gifted to you now that you understand your condition and are working to manage it in order to attain a better future.

3. Burnout. This causes all of us to lose the plot sometimes, whether we're ADHDers or not, so it shouldn't be a surprise that it's on the list. Whether it's due to overwork, over-worry, or situations outside of your control, if you're beginning to feel overloaded, it's time to take a breather and reset your mind and body. You have to discover what works best for you: a weekend in the woods, an afternoon on the beach, a luxuriant

bubble bath, or time with a good book. Taking time out to re-energize yourself and nourish the soul is as important as it gets. If the overload is more mental than physical, then the above will still help, but you can also complete a mind exercise to clear out the clutter from your brain. Mindfulness is excellent for this, and we'll talk about some of the incredible benefits of mindfulness in a later chapter. If mindfulness just isn't for you (but please do keep trying with it, as the rewards are incredibly advantageous), here is a simple but hugely beneficial pen-and-paper task you can complete:

On one side of a piece of paper, write down everything that's going on inside your mind that might be causing you stress or anxiety. Everything. Even small things like trying to remember you need to buy a new toothbrush. When you have that all written down, use the other side of the paper to organize every item into two lists. The first list is titled *Things I have no control over*, and the second list is *Things I have some control over*. For example, the fact that your aunt in Maine has a sprained ankle and can't walk the husky may be upsetting to you, but it is not something you have any control over. You can neither fix your aunt's ankle nor fly cross-country daily to walk the dog. That one has to go in the *Things I have no control over* column. On the other hand, the fact that your daughter is struggling with friendship groups at school is something you are able to help with, even if only on the scale of comforting and reassuring her. Of course, you may well want to do more than that, so this one goes in the *Things I have some control over* column. The tricky (but doable) part is to then let go of the things you cannot fix. You've acknowledged they are an issue, but you recognize that the solution is out of your hands (even with your visionary outlook!). The final step is to allocate three priorities on the list of things you can control. Though they may all seem like priorities in your head, when you have to categorize them on paper, you suddenly realize that you can probably make do with the same toothbrush for another week or two. For each of the three priorities, decide what action you need to take and give yourself a feasible timescale in which to achieve it. Then go make your world better. Once you tick something off the list, upgrade one of the other concerns and keep going.

4. Unnecessary risk-taking. Risk-taking in itself doesn't have to be a negative thing (as you'll see in chapter six: "Rewarding the risk-taker"), but there are risks, and there are *risks*. Destructive behavior is harmful to those around us as well as ourselves, and granting yourself permission to make ill-measured decisions is (as with self-medicating, below) only ever likely to reap short-lived rewards, if any at all. Yes, Icarus and Daedalus were on to something – they were indeed visionaries, but had Icarus heeded his father's advice (incidentally, his "significant other") instead of taking an unnecessary risk, he could have easily prevented tragedy. Listen to those you trust before making important decisions. Weigh up the pros and cons. Measured risk will get you to Sicily rather than

Davey Jones' Locker.

5. Self-medicating. This is as dangerous as it sounds but surprisingly common among those with ADHD. Turning to illicit drugs, cigarettes, and alcohol to calm the symptoms of ADHD and relax is something many will be able to relate to. Inevitably, it's the repercussions and after-effects of these habits that cause people to lose any sense of control they might have felt they achieved while self-medicating. This is something to avoid at all costs. If you feel you are susceptible to this false control mechanism, please seek advice and help from a medical professional. You can always fall back on some of the common support mechanisms above, which are more sustainable in terms of maintaining control: a significant other, prescribed medication, support groups, etc.

This is not a magic code. Having read this chapter, you won't instantly find you are able to control your chaotic ADHD symptoms perfectly. What I do hope is that with this knowledge you will be able to put some of these techniques into practice and, slowly but surely, increase the amount of time you feel in control.

What about the patterns then? Being in control is the foundation required in order to see them, and seeing them is part of your ADHD gift. Once your mind is settled and ordered, the beads of the kaleidoscope fall into place naturally, and the world becomes both more beautiful and more full of opportunity. Being able to communicate your vision, from a world perspective to a simple solution at work or at home, is what will provide you and those around you with abundant rewards.

3 UNLOCKING THE ENTREPRENEUR

It's no secret that ADHD is not a barrier to success – at least it shouldn't be by the time you're reading this. Numerous forerunners in the world of business credit their ADHD as a contributor to their success. As well as the aforementioned Sir Richard Branson and Paul Orfalea, case studies mention many other well-known company founders, such as David Neeleman (JetBlue) and Ingvar Kamprad (IKEA). Who else would have considered it plausible to make a fortune from customers-do-most-of-the-work-by-building-it-themselves furniture, other than a visionary with ADHD?

Neeleman is regularly quoted in the positive ADHD press as saying that he would refuse a "cure" for his ADHD if he were offered it. He says, "My ADD [a historical term for ADHD] brain naturally searches for better ways of doing things." In fact, people with ADHD are 300% more likely to become entrepreneurs than those without the diagnosis, and they are also more likely to succeed at it.

Being a visionary is just part of what makes ADHDers prone to entrepreneurial achievement; it's an essential trait which helps to sow the first seeds of entrepreneurship. Being an idea generator and looking at the world from different angle allows an ADHDer to spot gaps in the market, see a need that isn't being fulfilled, or visualize a better way of doing something.

Once the concept has been born, there are further characteristics common to ADHDers which help to ensure the idea is brought to fruition: hyperfocus, resilience, problem-solving abilities, creativity, risk tolerance, charisma, confidence, drive, and ambition. How to harness these skills and make them work for you is the focus of the rest of this guide. But first, let's look at how ADHD has helped some of the entrepreneurial trailblazers to succeed.

Learning from the Best

David Neeleman faced hordes of critics when he announced that his new company (JetBlue Airways) was going to be, "New York's new, low-fare, hometown airline." Venture capitalists backed out of the project, and the New York media was scathing in its condemnation. They didn't have the same vision as Neeleman. And look who's laughing now.

Neeleman has in fact founded four different airlines – in itself, evidence of his drive and ambition. When he was ejected from his post as CEO of JetBlue in 2008 following a spate of plane-groundings due to weather issues, he didn't sit back on his laurels and retire to the coast with the fortune he had already made by proving the non-believers wrong. Of course not – he has ADHD. He did what you'd expect any ADHDer to do, and defied the critics once more by setting up a new airline, largely based on the same model, but this time in Brazil. Brazil? Cue the naysayers once more rolling their eyes and predicting failure, but according to the Brazilian Civil Aviation Authority (ANAC), Azul ("Blue" in Portuguese) was the third largest airline in the country by 2015. The company received a reported investment of US$450million the same year.

"With the disorganization, procrastination, and inability to focus, and all the other bad things that come with ADHD, there also comes creativity and the ability to take risks," Neeleman has explained. "I knew I had strengths that other people didn't have, and my parents reminded me of them when my teachers didn't see them." What a remarkable validation of the benefit those "significant others" can have on an ADHDer's mindset.

He also recognizes his visionary ability: "I can distill complicated facts and come up with simple solutions. I can look out on an industry with all kinds of problems and say, 'How can I do this better?'"

It's no wonder that he values his ADHD so much. In fact, he feels so reliant on the traits his ADHD gives him that he has chosen to abstain from any traditional medication. "I'm afraid of taking drugs once, blowing a circuit, and then being like the rest of you." Clearly, Neeleman does see his ADHD as a superpower, and it's difficult to disagree with him.

The multi-billionaire founder of the IKEA furniture chain Ingvard Kamprad contends with the everyday challenges of both ADHD and dyslexia, and has stated that he adapted the inner workings of his business to compensate for these. Whilst he is less of an advocate for the ADHD advantage than Neeleman, it is impossible to interpret his company's vision without recognizing the inherent benefits his ADHD has provided.

"Only those who are asleep make no mistakes," Kamprad is famously quoted as saying. The propensity of the ADHDer for risk-taking and bravery is evident in this statement, as well as the buoyant confidence in the pursuit of goals and refusal to be knocked down permanently. In reality, Kamprad seems to be suggesting that being knocked down is a goal in itself: the lessons learned from failure are the building blocks for success. Thomas Edison, the inventor of the lightbulb, is another visionary rumored to have had ADHD (though this is obviously impossible to prove now). He had a similar philosophy: "I have not failed. I've just found 10,000 ways that don't work." It's impossible to deny the drive and determination clearly present in these minds.

Kamprad refuses to believe in the word "impossible," claiming it "has been and must remain deleted from our dictionary." His inclination towards entrepreneurship begain from a very young age, proving that even children with ADHD are capable of visionary thought and consequent achievement when given the right focus and encouragement to engage with their gifts. "I bought seeds for the garden and had great success with it, going around to all the houses in my village. After that year I could buy myself my first bicycle."

Born in 1926, yet still furthering his status as a "business magnate," Kamprad claims, "I don't have time for dying." Driven to remain productive, he urges his employees (whom he calls his co-workers) to not waste a moment of their time on this planet. "You can do so much in ten minutes' time. Ten minutes, once gone, are gone for good. Divide your life into ten-minute units and sacrifice as few of them as possible in meaningless activity." My non-ADHD brain frequently dismisses a ten-minute hiatus as impossible of "meaningful" activity. I'm more likely to indulge in a cup of tea than realize I could have edited half a chapter of a manuscript. Not that cups of tea are meaningless of course – I've already advocated the benefits of some time out as a way of rebalancing the soul – but I think Kamprad has a point which will resonate with many ADHDers. The ability to achieve something worthwhile in a small amount of time is a facility I truly wish I had (and something I can work on), but for an ADHDer, it's a natural instinct, as long as the activity innately appeals to their interests or pursuits.

Linked to the ability to hyperfocus is the persistent pursuit of "betterness," both parts of an ADHDer's set of skills that make entrepreneurial achievement more likely. I mention success a lot, but Kamprad warns against any goal being the ultimate destination: "The most dangerous poison is the feeling of achievement. The antidote is to every evening think what can be done better tomorrow." He adds, "Happiness is not reaching your goal. Happiness is being on the way." I'd like to think that what I mean by success is exactly what Kamprad refers to as happiness.

Being the Best

How do we learn from those who have used their ADHD powers for good?

Well, let's break it all down and analyze the lessons Neeleman and Kamprad can teach us.

Don't listen to the naysayers

This is possibly the most encouraging part of Neeleman's story. Others couldn't see his vision, but he didn't let that stop him. Remember that ADHD allows you to see possibilities outside of most people's horizontal logic. Neeleman didn't say he "thought" he had strengths others didn't possess. He said he "knew." Trust your research and your instinct. You still need to do the math, but chances are it'll add up.

Keep going, whatever the obstacles

For Neeleman, losing his position as CEO of JetBlue could have meant the end (and still a successful one) of his aviation dreams. Kamprad could have given in to societal norms and retired with his fortune. Neither chose the easy path. They could have, but they didn't. Neither actually view obstacles as a negative, but rather as lessons and knowledge to be gathered along the journey. Both have persevered and gone on to achieve even more despite both the naysayers and the obstacles. Have the conviction to keep chasing the dream; it'll be worth it.

Carve your own path

This is all about confidence and owning your diagnosis. For Neeleman, it means foregoing the typical medication route. Whilst I would not push anyone to follow this path arbitrarily simply because it works for him, that does not mean there isn't a valuable lesson here. Neeleman has learnt how to manage his ADHD without medication. The key to that is learning how to manage your ADHD effectively. For most, this will include medication; for some, it may not. Rather than trumpeting ADHD as the hero of his story, Kamprad instead suggests he manages his ADHD by compensating for it (along with his dyslexia). Compensating does not inherently suggest that sacrifices are being made. It rather means that he, too, has found what works for him when it comes to successfully managing his symptoms. It's about working out the ADHD journey that's right for you. As I've already mentioned, this may take some trial and error, but if you persevere, the rewards will be rich.

Pursue self-betterment

It's not over until the fat lady sings. And then it's still not over. Both Kamprad and Neeleman have reinvented themselves and their ideas, continually searching for better ways to do things. It's a challenge IKEA is famous for: how can we make something that should be complicated beautifully simple? Finding an answer is great, but as with ideas, there is always more than one. Perfection is the pursuit of fools, for once you feel you've achieved it, you stop learning. One thing we can all be certain of is that perfection is actually a myth. Betterment, however, is an entirely worthy endeavor. Do as Kamprad suggests and ensure as many of your ten-minute slots as possible are geared towards this.

Embrace your ability to hyperfocus

More on how you can achieve this later, but it's worth noting here how relentless Neeleman and Kamprad were in their determination. Getting the job done involves commitment and hard work, neither of which are things ADHDers are afraid of. Concentrate ferociously on the task at hand at any one moment – research and development, sales, admin, marketing, joint ventures, or whatever it is – and you're already a step ahead. Even better, ADHDers thrive on multitasking – something "the rest of us" are inclined to liken to plate spinning or juggling: precarious activities which usually involve failure. Not so for the ADHD brain. Capitalize on this advantage and unleash the entrepreneur within.

I'm not recommending that any ADHDer reading this should quit their day job and launch a start-up tomorrow. Becoming a successful entrepreneur takes time and endeavor, but it is worth noting that on average ADHDers who are employed rather than working for themselves tend to earn 33% less than non-ADHDers. Playing the ADHD brain game right means refusing to become one of these statistics. Use this guide to master your symptoms and to make them work for you. Whether you become an entrepreneur or not is irrelevant. You have to follow your own path towards whatever you deem success to be.

4 BIG PICTURE, SMALL DETAILS

This might sound like a paradox. Usually, people are either good at being able to see the bigger picture, or they are better at focusing on the small details. A typical assumption might be that a CEO has the bigger picture as his or her focus, while the PA is great at concentrating on the smaller details and making sure the CEO is where he or she is supposed to be at the right time and with the right papers. This is one more area where ADHDers have a distinct advantage, as they are capable of doing both incredibly well.

I've already mentioned that ADHDers love to multitask. The satisfaction experienced with this, alongside the focus they can potentially muster, helps them to perceive microscopic details and notice things others would miss, making them a valuable asset in many situations. Combined with this is an ability to maintain a sense of the bigger picture and to therefore see how all the pieces of the puzzle fit together.

Take my neighbor's son as an example. Remember that he is still far off becoming a teenager, and therefore even further away from becoming an adult capable of educating himself and fully comprehending his ADHD diagnosis. He does recognize that he is different though: different to my kids and to the others in his family. Of course, he plays happily with all – more so now that he consciously practices mindfulness techniques – but he still has moments when his ADHD marks him as different and, in several cases, more detail-oriented than the rest of us.

The other week, he was playing with my two, and they were in the middle of the construction of what promised to be an enormous sandcastle. They had laid foundations of strong wet sand (I was already impressed by their advanced thinking!) and were beginning to build turret-shaped outer walls using their buckets. My two were merrily knocking the sand out of the containers, lining castle after castle along the edge of the outer walls. My neighbor's child was doing the same on the opposing side. I hadn't noticed any issue with the game, but suddenly my neighbor's son was wailing. "What's the matter?" I asked while my own children paused in their endeavors and joined me in looking surprised and quizzical. "What's happened?" I could see no beach critters around, he didn't seem to be in any kind of pain, and his towers appeared fully intact rather than ravaged by wind, wave or wayward feet.

Once he had remembered how to calm himself down and had his breathing under control, he was able to explain that my own children weren't building the sandcastle "properly." I inspected the progress of the building, which seemed pretty much like any ordinary (if somewhat ambitious) sandcastle to me. In fact, my kids had covered nearly three times the ground he had – well, there were two of them – and so I thought they were doing quite well. But it turned out that therein lay the problem.

While his upturned buckets were neatly arranged in a uniform line, shoulder to shoulder like soldiers, those placed by my own kids were rather more haphazardly positioned, sometimes a few inches apart, sometimes one a little more forward or behind the other.

"We can't build on top on top of those!" he said, pointing. "The sandcastle won't stand up properly." And of course, he was absolutely right. The vision he had of the completed, monumental sandcastle was an impossibility given the slapdash nature of my children's engineering skills.

Once I'd appeased the situation, and bolstered my children's demolished sandcastle-building skills, I had time to reflect on what had just happened. Not only had my neighbor's son been able to notice the minor details of the mal-constructed wall, but he had also been able to step back and see exactly how it was going to impact the bigger picture. Impressive, and entirely in keeping with his ADHD diagnosis. What a valuable skill this will be for him in the future! I can only imagine the palatial structures he will be creating in a few years' time.

The amazing thing is, despite his youth, he was able to recognize what my children (and indeed myself) could not. The reason for this is simple: he cared about the sandcastle; he cared about his vision.

When an ADHDer is invested in a project, little will stop them from seeing it through, and this includes holding a microscope up to the smallest of details as well as appreciating how the bigger picture is likely to play out. So why had my neighbor's son allowed my kids to build so much before pointing out their error? Simple: hyperfocus.

Zoning Out or Zoning In?

Hyperfocus is possibly the last thing someone would expect to be attainable for an ADHDer. How often have we heard ADHD described as "the inability to focus" or "the inability to sit still?" In fact, ADHD is more accurately described as the inability to regulate focus and attention. This is because once someone with ADHD tunes in to something that fully engages them, they are capable of focus on a level many of us will never fully appreciate. Conversely, when presented with something that they find uninteresting or uninspiring, it is incredibly difficult for an ADHDer to concentrate, however much they may be trying.

This ability to hyperfocus is perhaps responsible for the frustration often felt by "outsiders" when presented with someone who potentially has ADHD. Can you remember a teacher or a work superior ever saying, "Well, you can apply yourself when you want to…" almost as though it's an accusation and a suggestion that you're lazy or discourteous? If only it were that simple. But the problem isn't that an ADHDer doesn't want to, it's that unless they are invested in the topic, outcome, or reward, their brain can't process the value of finding focus, however hard the person responsible for the brain might try. Exercises on how to convince your brain to pay better attention under such circumstances will follow later, but for now, I want to dwell on the phenomenon of the flip side.

If I had to select just one of the ADHD gifts that I really felt was closest to a superpower, then it would be a tough call between being a visionary and (properly managed) hyperfocus. Although it isn't a scientifically recognized "symptom" of ADHD, it is widely accepted as a manifestation or side effect. Simply put, hyperfocus involves an ADHDer becoming so completely engrossed in an activity or pursuit that everything else around them seems to disappear. They become entirely fixated on the task at hand, whether that's finishing a work report, playing a video game, starting up a business, or indeed, building a sandcastle. Whatever the activity is, it receives unbroken attention – sometimes to the detriment of all else.

Kathleen Nadeau, a clinical psychologist in D.C. and a specialist in attention "disorders," cites a case in her book *Adventures in Fast Forward* of a woman with ADHD who was so hyperfocused on a paper she was writing that she had no idea her house was burning down around her! For those of us unlikely to ever experience what real hyperfocus is like, this is pretty difficult to believe, but Nadeau writes, "She had missed the sirens and all the commotion and was finally discovered by firemen, working contentedly in her room while the kitchen at the back of the house was engulfed in flames." Fortunately, the woman was safely evacuated, with no harm to herself or the paper, but the same cannot be said about the house.

Cast your mind back and consider if you've ever been accused of "zoning out" or not listening to someone who has repeatedly been trying to get your attention. Is it possible that rather than being "zoned out" you were in fact "zoned in" and hyperfocused on whatever other activity was on hand?

Aside from letting your house burn down around you, there are other negative implications to hyperfocus, but these can be easily managed once known. Most obviously, the downfall of hyperfocus is the potential to neglect other things in your life: people, chores, responsibilities. Most of these tend to be vital parts of a healthy life, so finding ways to ensure this doesn't happen is pretty important.

The first step is to learn what activities usually draw you into a state of hyperfocus. Once you have worked this out, utilize things like diaries and planners, phone reminders, to-do lists, alarm clocks, and timers to ensure you don't get completely lost in your world of hyperfocus. Medication is another potential solution to avoid finding yourself overwhelmingly lost in a hyperfocused state. It's also useful to ask yourself if you have any other pressing engagements or responsibilities before entering into an activity you recognize as one where you're likely to hyperfocus. Twenty minutes before guests are due to arrive may not be an appropriate time to zone in, so be conscious of this. Of course, if you manage to align your vocation with your typical hyperfocus activities, then you're on to a winner!

The benefits of this near-superpower probably don't need spelling out, but just in case you feel the need to sell this skill to a potential employer, romantic partner, or the man on the street wondering why you've spent the past hour staring through a camera lens trying to get the perfect shot of a rare bird, here you go:

1.   Meeting tight deadlines
2.   Boosting self-esteem through hyperfocus-related achievement
3.   Improved relationships with romantic

partners/children, if time spent with them becomes hyperfocused

4.   Status as someone who "gets things done"

5.   Increased opportunity to invent, discover and innovate – statistics suggest the more hours spent on something, the more likely you are to finding a rewarding outcome

Harnessing your hyperfocus and properly managing it means it truly can be a valuable part of your individuality.

Putting the Puzzle Together

With well-managed hyperfocus added to your armory, I hope you are beginning to see how your set of skills makes ADHD seem more like a gift than a "disorder." Discovering and working on strengths such as this can help to make you an individual with ADHD rather than a "sufferer" or one of a matching set created from a mythical ADHD mold.

It's not just the small details and bigger picture of the world around you that you should tune your ADHD advantage into. You also need to apply the same principle to understanding yourself and what ADHD means for you. Putting the pieces of the puzzle together will help it all make sense.

My mom is a jigsaw puzzle fanatic. She has two wardrobe-sized cupboards she bought especially to store her burgeoning collection in. They're all 1000 pieces, and they get rotated in and out of the cupboards on a fast-moving conveyor belt (metaphorically that is, she isn't that crazy). As new ones arrive from the internet (on a weekly basis), those she has completed get farmed out to a retirement home.

She has a system to maximize her efficiency for completing a jigsaw that seems genius to me. Now that I've seen it, I don't know why you'd ever do a puzzle any other way. The method must have been created by an ADHDer, as far as I'm concerned. It's super simple too. She has "sorting boxes," so as she initially goes through the 1000 puzzle pieces, each gets put in a box according to what's on it. One box for edge pieces; one box for people; one box for trees; one box for buildings; one box for sky; and so on. One mammoth sorting session, and she's set to complete the puzzle in record time because everything is already compartmentalized.

Life needs to be like that too. But the metaphor goes further. Yes, she'll stick with convention and build the edges first – everything needs some sort of structure. But after that, it isn't a case of working from the edges inward. Instead, she focuses on the details – just like an ADHDer can, and should. The puzzle pieces don't go anywhere near the actual puzzle board until enough of the section – a group of people, a tree or a bridge – is pieced together in its sorting box first. By focusing on the details separately, she has huge sections pieced together in no time. Then she steps back and looks at the bigger picture, considering where she is going to place each of the detailed sections within the picture. Before you know it, the puzzle is put together not piece by piece, but chunk by chunk, until just the awkward filler bits (usually dark trees or sky) are left. The beautiful scene materializes as the small details, one by one, become part of the bigger picture.

44

As an ADHDer, you have the innate ability to apply this principle to everything you do because the small details grab your attention and make sense to you in a way that others may not appreciate. But, more importantly, as an ADHDer, your first puzzling challenge is to piece together the details that make you, you. Some of these will relate to ADHD, and hopefully, this guide will be opening your eyes to how special these pieces and details are. Others will have nothing to do with your ADHD-wired brain at all, but they are just as relevant to your individuality. Once you start connecting the pieces, you'll see how well your ADHD fits with those other parts of you. Pay close attention to where these sections join; chances are you'll find your hyperfocus loves these parts of your own, unique picture.

The Art of Stepping Back

One final piece of advice for this chapter. As you build the puzzle – and the many puzzles you will come across once you have figured out your own – remember the importance of stepping back and considering how the sections work together to make the best, most coherent picture possible. Perspective is really important. Just because two sections contain blue flowers, there's no sense in ramming them together when they just won't fit. Giving yourself the time and distance to work out what belongs where will be worth it in the end, because once there's one piece in the wrong place, everything falls apart (mom always blames dad for putting those pieces in!).

This is a great point to introduce you to the brilliance of mindfulness and meditation – two of my favorite passions and ultimate pleasures. Both of these practices are an excellent way of stilling the mind and allowing yourself to step back from the detail. Sometimes, the detail can be all-consuming, and it would be utterly exhausting to live in a constant state of hyperfocus.

Mindfulness and meditation also have the benefit of nurturing your emotional intelligence and allowing you to understand your own needs and responses better, positively impacting those around you. All this while stilling the mind and giving you some peace from constantly feeling like a wound spring. Mindfulness and meditation time can also include exercises aimed at improving your self-compassion – something ADHDers are known to lack because society makes such a fuss about the negative impact of the condition on the rest of the world.

There's been an explosion in the practice of meditation and mindfulness over the past few years (hooray!), and as a consequence, there's plenty of literature out there for you to access. I strongly recommend these disciplines as my experience (and that of those I've introduced to them) suggests you won't regret it for a second! Short sessions of mindfulness and/or meditation every day – and I mean every single day – for as little as ten minutes can make a wealth of difference to your world. Remember Kamprad's mandate to use every ten minutes you have wisely? I can't think of a better way to heed his advice.

Mindfulness begins with breathing techniques, which allow you to slow down the world around you or, perhaps more relevantly, the world inside your head. By training yourself to focus on just one simple thing – your breathing – you begin to train your mind to shut out the noise and chaos. A word of warning: it takes time and practice! And it might require even more time and practice depending on the type and severity of your ADHD. Allow yourself to fail, but once again, use your tenacious capacity for perseverance to help you to get there in the end. As a short introduction, here is a simple breathing exercise you can practice. Read the guidance through completely before trying it out.

Mindful Breathing
The first thing you need to do is to learn to "ground" yourself. This doesn't mean getting locked in your room by your parents, but the reasoning behind the term is very similar! Start by making sure you are sitting comfortably in a quiet space. You should have a straight back – not slouched, relaxed shoulders, and your feet should be flat on the floor. Rest your forearms and hands on your lap. I prefer to have my palms facing upward, but do whatever is comfortable for you.

Once you are comfortable, close your eyes.

First of all, be conscious of your feet and their connection to the ground. Then of your body resting on the chair. Use that feeling to help yourself to feel secure and steady – in other words, "grounded."

Take a slow, deep breath in. Not a normal breath, but a really deep one. Our typical, everyday breathing uses only a small part of our lungs; mindful breathing helps you use your full lung capacity. With a normal breath, you will feel and see your chest rise and fall with the intake and exhalation of breath. With a full, deep breath, your diaphragm will also expand. Your diaphragm is beneath your chest, just above your stomach. If it helps, rest your palm there and try to feel it expanding and contracting with your breath. I find it easier to breathe in through both my nose and my mouth when I want to take a full breath.

Once you are confident that you are breathing deeply, start to control the length of your breathing. Aim to breathe in to the count of five, and out to the count of ten. Each time you fully exhale, renew your sense of connection with the floor and chair.

The next stage is to breathe in for the count of five, hold your breath for the count of three, and then exhale for the count of ten.

During each held second, be conscious of your entire body and how it feels in that exact moment of space and time.

You'll be amazed at how quickly this simple exercise can help to still your mind and focus your concentration. Just a few minutes of this every day, and you'll notice the benefit it is having on the rest of your day too.

There are ways of furthering the exercise, to focus on your emotions and release worries and stress with each exhalation, but you can build up to these slowly. The first and most important step is to become fully conscious of the mechanism of breathing in a particular place in time.

There are also some excellent (and some not so good, but find what works for you) guided meditations out there. These are typically visualizations that begin by focusing on your breathing and then walking you through an imagined scenario in your mind's eye. I've found these can be excellent stress relievers, and you can find specific guided meditations for all sorts of things: conquering fear; helping with grief; coping with anxiety or depression; and even ones specifically for helping to calm the ADHD mind. They are available for kids as well as adults, and will have a wonderful impact on your general well-being – at least that's what everyone I've introduced them to says!

These meditation and mindfulness exercises are just one way of helping you to step back and consider the bigger picture, separating yourself from the onslaught of a hyperactive mind. They are also really useful in helping to avoid the burnout that so often causes ADHDers to lose control of their symptoms. Balance this big picture perspective with attention to the small details and your kaleidoscope view will flourish.

5 CREATIVITY AT YOUR FINGERTIPS

The scientific research to support this theory is thorough, modern, and overwhelming. I'm not going to start using scientific phrases that took me weeks to get my head around (you're welcome!), but let me say this: psychologists, analysts, MDs, PhDs, cognitive neuroscientists – you name them – believe the research points to creativity being something ADHDers have a natural inclination to achieve in.

The overlapping symptoms in those with ADHD and incredibly creative people include:

- Inattention and daydreaming
- Sensation seeking
- Inability to finish projects
- Hyperactivity
- Enthusiasm and playfulness
- Difficult temperament
- Deficient social skills
- Academic underachievement
- Hypersensitivity to stimulation
- Mood swings
- Use of imagery in problem-solving

While you may now be aware of how to manage some of the symptoms that have a more negative interpretation, that doesn't necessarily mean you'll be stifling any of the creative juices that will naturally flood your system as an ADHDer.

It's not about right and left sides of the brain

either, nor does stimulant medication suppress creativity as was once assumed. A 2009 double-blind, placebo-controlled study found that whilst stimulant medication often improved the memory test function of ADHDers (known in scientific studies as "convergent thought"), the "divergent thought" processes (ones requiring creativity rather than straight answers from memory) were not impacted negatively in any way. Sounds like a win-win, right?

Even more significantly, medication aside, studies have also shown that ADHDers are not only more creative but also more likely to achieve with their creative endeavors than non-ADHDers. Given the number of entrepreneurial successes with ADHDers at the helm, this makes complete sense. The same studies also support what we learnt about ADHDers as ideas generators; they prefer to come up with ideas, while non-ADHDers prefer to filter problems and build on the ideas of others.

Another parallel that can be drawn between creative people and those with ADHD is that they all have difficulty quieting the parts of the brain which control imaginative thought – hence the inattentive-type daydreaming, the ideas, and the vast number of ADHDers in the arts industry.

On top of the arts-connected ADHD-diagnosed celebrities mentioned in chapter one (Justin Timberlake, Karina Smirnoff, Will Smith, Joan Rivers, Emma Watson, and Ty Pennington, in case you need a recap), there are plenty of other creatives who are commonly listed as demonstrating the trademark signs of ADHD, including: Ansel Adams, Anne Bancroft, Beethoven, Hans Christian Anderson, Lewis Carroll, Leonardo da Vinci, Walt

Disney, Cher, Thomas Edison, Robin Williams, Henry Winkler, and Stevie Wonder. It's a pretty cool list to be part of, isn't it?

Patrick McKenna, host and actor (ADD and Loving it), suggests that Hollywood is a natural home for those with ADHD. As it is somewhere unusual and creative, people feel more accepted and free to express themselves without reproach. Of course, that doesn't mean that it's impossible for an ADHDer to feel at home working outside of the arts; there are plenty of ways you can channel your creativity.

Painting by Numbers

As we've learnt, ADHDers prefer an alternative approach to most things, and the same can be said for the way they might choose to use their creative predilections. Whilst careers involving art and design, photography, writing, music, performance, and comedy are all worthy pursuits ADHDers can excel in, there's no blueprint or expectation for you to use your creativity in this way. Painting by numbers simply isn't an ADHDer's style!

Consider also how creative thinking applies in the business world. Kamprad certainly utilizes a creative management style and a non-conformist philosophy that has worked wonders for him, his company, and his employees. Entrepreneurial endeavors necessitate creative and inventive thought processes. Solving problems in the workplace can often be achieved with more creative thought than logic. Marketing careers (not just in terms of the design aspect) benefit from a creative outlook, and management who can find creative ways to engage and motivate their staff are more likely to avoid employee apathy and lackluster performance.

One of the researchers goes as far as suggesting that the key to making education work better for ADHD children is to make creativity a pathway for learning rather than just an outcome of it. The exact same principle can be applied to any workplace, whether you're looking to engage ADHD staff or find ways of utilizing your own ADHD creative advantage.

My ADHD novelist friend believes his hyperfocus is closely linked to his creativity. When he reaches a hyperfocused state of creativity, he says it feels like his "blood is running with raw adrenaline." It's a natural high he depends on in order to "write books much faster than most – working like a well-honed machine." Though he credits the ADHD drug Ritalin with helping him to maintain his ultra-productive state, he is clearly in the same camp as Neeleman and wouldn't change his status as an ADHDer for anything. For him, working in the arts industry, it's what gives him the creative edge.

Whichever industry you are a part of – or decide to become a part of – your creative bent is an asset which need never be tamed. Refuse to be constrained by expectations, abandon the numbered canvas, and trust your creative instincts.

6 REWARDING THE RISK-TAKER

This is one of the aspects associated with ADHD typically shrouded in negativity. And wrongly so! It is true that the majority of people walking this planet are risk-averse rather than risk-tolerant, but that doesn't (or shouldn't) dictate that risk-taking is an undesirable action.

Unfortunately, too many people focus on the extremes involved in risk-taking, that is to say, the ultra-high-risk activities involving personal danger or loss. It's true that ADHDers are more prone to addiction then non-ADHDers; it's the fault of a low level of dopamine, and the consequent thrilling rush received when it suddenly floods the system. But clearly, an ADHDer's high-risk behavior doesn't necessarily have to involve illicit drugs, cigarettes, alcohol, gambling, or any of those recreational activities that are rightly understood by society at large as condemnable. And let's be honest, it isn't just ADHDers who are likely to drive a little too fast, spontaneously book a bungee jump, or jump out of an airplane at 10,000 feet above ground (hopefully strapped to a parachute).

In fact, involving yourself in high-risk activities is not recognized as a symptom of ADHD, but is rather something heavily associated with ADHDers based on years of scientific research. This means ADHDers are simply more prone to high-risk activities that non-ADHDers, not that they inherently feel the need to take their own life in their hands. This proclivity is due to a few reasons, which are more directly connected with the symptoms of ADHD.

What the research primarily shows is that ADHDers are more likely to underestimate the risk involved in any particular situation, and it is this, rather than actual thrill-seeking, which often marks them out as risk-takers. They aren't unable to recognize risk, but will regularly misinterpret the level of risk or underplay the potential consequences of the risk. While non-ADHDers will assess preventative and precautionary measures, ADHDers are less likely to consider this necessary.

At the same time, earlier studies conducted in the 1980s suggest that those who do demonstrate thrill-seeking behavior do so because of a lack of stimulation received elsewhere. ADHD children under-aroused by their studies or play will consequently search for more engaging activities, which inevitably opens them up to a broader set of experiences, including those closer to the ends of the risk spectrum. While this sort of behavior is more likely to diminish as ADHDers develop greater social maturity, the ability to accurately assess risk fluctuates less, unless of course, the ADHDer sources either experience or education to counteract that.

Sink or Swim

The advantages of being more risk-tolerant become quite clear once you remove the inaccurate focus on the more dangerous "extreme" behaviors. The fearlessness required to take that extra step compared to others is what gets you (and your business) further. The great explorers of the world would never have discovered this country if they hadn't been prepared to flout the level of risk involved and set sail into the unknown.

That "unknown" is what creates appetite for the ADHDer; rather than being pragmatically cautious about unchartered territory, they are instead excited about the prospects of new discovery which lie within its scope. And as we've already seen, an excited ADHDer can be unstoppable!

Yes, there can be a bit of a "sink or swim" mentality, but the ADHDer who sinks will undoubtedly find a survival strategy, haul themselves out of the water, reassess, and then throw themselves back in again and again until they become Michael Phelps.

Business mogul and ADHDer Richard Branson cites risk-taking as "the only ticket to experiencing new and exciting things." Famed for his love of hot-air ballooning and his mission to head into space, Branson is guilty of the extreme risk behaviors even most ADHDers would recognize the danger in. But for him, pushing those boundaries is part of experiencing life to the full.

His Virgin website even includes a list of his ten favorite quotes on risk, demonstrating that it's the perceived benefit from risk-taking that makes the potential endangerment worthwhile.

As with Edison and Kamprad, Branson sees failure as a learning experience rather than a negative, and each new challenge as an opportunity rather than a risk. Here are his top five quotes on risk:

5.   "When you take risks you learn that there will be times when you succeed and there will be

times when you fail, and both are equally important."
– Ellen DeGeneres

4. "There is freedom waiting for you,
On the breezes of the sky,
And you ask 'What if I fall?'
Oh but my darling,
What if you fly?" – Erin Hanson

3. "I am always doing that which I cannot do, in order that I may learn how to do it." – Pablo Picasso

2. "Don't be afraid to take a big step. You can't cross a chasm in two small jumps."– David Lloyd George

And finally, a quote from a poem which has always inspired me and my non-ADHD brain to tread new ground:

1. "Two roads diverged in a wood … I took the one less travelled by, and that has made all the difference." – Robert Frost

Wearing Water Wings

I am an advocate of measured risk-taking. That is, I believe it wise to embrace some risk and to grow and benefit accordingly – either personally or professionally – but I also believe it worthwhile to manage the risk in order to avoid unredeemable loss. Perhaps it's my financial background talking, but risk management is huge in today's business world, and the same principles can provide some fundamental strategies for ADHDers who are conscious that they veer towards the more extreme risk behaviors.

These approaches to risk can be broken down into five basic categories: Risk Acceptance, Risk Avoidance, Risk Transference, Risk Mitigation and Risk Exploitation. A savvy ADHDer will assess which is the best strategy to employ at any one given time, and even the task of considering a strategy makes the ADHDer more likely to achieve a rewarding outcome – whether they do indeed take the risk or not.

Risk Acceptance

This option is perfectly viable for small risks which bear little life-changing outcomes. It's really a do-nothing and carry-on approach! Basically, having assessed the risk, you deem it small enough to ignore and pursue the behavior anyway. The trick is to know when to use it and when to move to a different strategy. ADHDers are likely to employ this wisely if they also get to grips with Risk Mitigation.

Risk Avoidance

Risk Avoidance is the opposite of Risk Acceptance. This involves completely changing your intentions so that the assessed risk is removed entirely. Examples might include not accepting that first cigarette, holidaying at the beach or the city instead of in the Columbian Jungle, or taking a time out instead of telling your boss exactly what you think of his new marketing strategy! If you can pause for just half a second and try to evaluate the true measure of risk involved, you may find this strategy useful in particularly emotional or fraught situations.

Risk Transference

This is a less commonly used principle in business, perhaps with the exception of insurance practices. However, it could be extremely useful on a personal level too (and of course we have personal insurances as part of our everyday life, such as life insurance and health insurance). Trusting a "significant other" to advise you if such insurances are required could be hugely beneficial. Don't be afraid to run risks past those you trust, and be wary of false risk transference: just because you transfer the responsibility of your safe descent to the skydiving instructor and the parachute, it's still you jumping out of the plane and falling 10,000 feet! Consequently, it's still your risk to take.

Risk Mitigation

Here lies the golden chalice of risk management. This is the most commonly employed strategy, and the good news is that it's likely to appeal to the risk-tolerant (and therefore ADHDers) because it means you still get to take the risk. Risk mitigation is possibly best described as "damage limitation." It works because it allows you to take the risk, but you've also enacted some control measures on how damaging the potential outcome could be. This is the ADHDer's water wings. Leaping into the water before taking swimming lessons is one thing; leaping into the water before taking swimming lessons while wearing water wings is another. While the risk-averse might be clutching the side of the pool or crying in the changing rooms, you've made it to the deep end and are still afloat. Because you chose the water wings to mitigate the risk, you did not sink to the bottom of the pool, choke on the water, have a panic attack, rely on the lifeguard to haul you out, or, worst case scenario, drown.

Learning how to mitigate risk sensibly without denying yourself the opportunity to progress beyond previous limitations, to discover, explore, and innovate is best done by having a team around you that you trust. And (surprise surprise!) self-education about the risks involved as well as prospective mitigation devices will mean that you're making the wisest decision you can.

Risk Exploitation

This strategy could be a natural instinct for ADHDers who are more likely to focus on the viable benefits of a risk than the pitfalls. The difficulty here lies in trusting yourself to recognize if the risk is indeed only a positive one or if it is outweighed by potential hazards. This is where your trusted team and self-education come in. Of course, if the risk does turn out to be potentially positive (such as spending the rest of your life with someone you love), then risk exploitation means doing everything you can to make that risk happen. Schmooze with the prospective in-laws! Buy the ring!

Taking risks is not inherently a bad thing. Taking a measured risk will increase your chances of winning the game. Dice and cards are unpredictable. Only play the tables where the odds are in your favor, or the reward dwarfs the risk.

7 MASTERING YOUR ENERGY

I've already mentioned my ADHD novelist friend (expect more about him later too); he makes a great case study because he's so positive about his ADHD diagnosis, even though he only got diagnosed at forty-eight. He likes to think of himself as an ADHD champion and was probably one of the biggest inspirations for this book. When I asked him what his favorite things about being an ADHDer were, his first response was emphatic: "It's the astonishing amount of energy! It's not normal energy; it's hyper, raw, untamed, wild rumpus energy!" Yes, he used those exact words – I have them recorded as proof! "Raw, untamed, wild rumpus energy." Wowsers. Sounds amazing, right?

Yet all too often it's the energy attributed to ADHDers that causes the most violent negative response. Children are constantly required to sit still and not fidget (a hugely unnatural thing for any child to do, never mind an ADHD child), and adults are largely treated the same way. Those struggling to contain their enormous amount of "raw, untamed, wild rumpus energy" are criticized for being disruptive or distracting, or worse, they are ironically reprimanded for not paying attention – which is very often not the case as the fidgeting is more likely to help them to concentrate.

The hyperactive-impulsive type is more likely to struggle with their unbridled energy, whilst the inattentive type is the one who will be staring out of the window while mentally playing baseball or winning an Oscar. Fortunately, in the more modern era of positive ADHD research, it has become very clear that ADHDers (of all types) are more able to focus when they are allowed to fidget or – better still – channel their frenetic energy into a mindless activity which distracts the part of the mind that wants them to be active, so that they can better focus on the task at hand. More on that later in the chapter.

The point is, the negative press brigade have spent years making the wrong kind of fuss out of the incredible energy ADHDers possess because it was misunderstood for so long. If you've been diagnosed with ADHD, then chances are you've had a discussion with your doctor about the recommended medications available to help you manage your ADHD symptoms. And what umbrella term is used for the most common ADHD medications? That's right, "stimulants" (ten out of ten if you didn't previously know, but remembered from chapter one!).

It might seem somewhat bizarre to be treating people who display excessive amounts of energy with a stimulant drug. But what the stimulants actually do is increase the availability of certain chemicals in the brain which help it to work more efficiently. Taking medication doesn't therefore stunt your energy or shut down your senses, but rather, once you find the right sort of medication and dosage for you, it helps your brain to make better decisions about how to use this energy. The novelist swears by his Ritalin saying that the diagnosis and consequent medication was a "game-changer," increasing his productivity beyond levels he previously thought possible.

Of course, I wholeheartedly recommend that you follow any advice from your doctor about the course of medication you take. But it would be remiss of me not to mention the many naturopathic and complementary options available to help with managing ADHD symptoms too. As with any "non-traditional" or "non-western" medication, it's important that you discuss your use of these options with your doctor to ensure that there are no possible conflicts or side effects when combining these with any other medication you may be taking.

I've already given you some ideas about the benefits of meditation and mindfulness for stilling the mind. These are also excellent for finding "body stillness" too. Having the energy of a puppy or a child on Christmas morning is brilliant (most of the time), but there can also be occasions where taking a time out from freneticism is a welcome relief. Both meditation and mindfulness will give you a peaceful space for your mind, body, and soul to regroup and recharge. I urge you to do some further research on these practices and to reap the consequent rewards. Closely related to these complementary therapies is the use of yoga. As a self-confessed yoga-nut (and self-trained yogi), I can't recommend this enough as a way of centering your energy, focusing the mind, and feeling in control. Introduce yoga into your regular lifestyle, and you'll soon be shouting from the rooftops about how incredible it is!

Further to that, there are many advocates of therapies like acupuncture and aromatherapy to "treat" the excessive energies of ADHD and help you to effectively control and focus it in the preferred direction. Whilst little scientific study has been done on the effect of acupuncture on ADHDers, it is a treatment used by many to help achieve greater internal balance between the yin and the yang in the body. It is believed that ADHD is related to a yang dominance in various key areas of the body, and that treatment with acupuncture can help to reset this. It's not an option for the needle-phobic, but it's far less invasive and painful than you might imagine! In fact, my personal experience of acupuncture has been an entirely positive and entirely pain-free one. It's worth noting that the acupuncture treatment for ADHD in children typically involves using the ears, which minimizes any chance of pain or personal space invasion. If you're more interested in using acupuncture as a way of treating ADHD, then please do seek out reputable local practitioners – there will be many to choose from! – and have a full consultation before deciding if this is a route for you. Remember also to speak to your regular doctor about including this in your personal treatment plan.

Aromatherapy is another complementary treatment widely used to treat ADHD both in children and adults. Below is a summary of the most beneficial oils to use and for what purpose. Again, if this appeals to you, please conduct further research and be sure to follow the instructions on administering essential oils carefully. They are not to be taken orally but are usually used with a diffuser and dispensed into the air around you to be inhaled, or they can be rubbed onto the body. Both methods require dilution, typically of just a 1-2% concentration. I'm a huge fan of aromatherapy as a treatment for all sorts of ailments, and whilst I haven't personally used these oils to specifically treat

ADHD myself, I can attest to the fact that they certainly "do what it says on the tin."

Aromatherapy oils for ADHD

Roman chamomile – soothes and comforts
Lavender – calms and helps to reduce anxiety
Mandarin – quiets (particularly when used with lavender)
Ylang ylang – sedates and calms the emotions
Vetiver – calms, while also focusing the mind
Frankincense – supports the immune system
Patchouli – soothes the nervous system
Cilantro – controls heavy metal toxins (commonly found in excess in ADHD children)
Cedar wood – stimulates thought and mental synergy
Rosemary – improves concentration and memory (especially good when studying)
Cypress oil – stabilizes thought processes and emotional reactions

Your energy is one of the most significant advantages of ADHD. All the above medicinal and therapeutic suggestions are meant to help you harness and channel this energy so that it is working for you and not against you. Use them wisely and become the master of this indefatigable force.

Running Round in Circles

Once you have found your perfect route to harnessed energy, there is little that can stop you from achieving whatever you set your mind to. But without a specific focus for this energy, you may still find yourself running round in circles rather than towards a specific goal. There's nothing intrinsically wrong with running round in circles – athletes do it all the time! – but if you can turn what was once a series of random or endless circles into a spiral (that is circles which hone in to a specific point), then you're on to a winner.

It's therefore important to know what your goals are, and setting these out formally – with your partner as part of the discussion – provides an excellent beginning to this process. Write down what you are working towards in all aspects of your life – family, relationship, work, fitness, etc. – and actively plan what you are going to do to achieve your goals. A SMART plan will help to ensure that your energy is permanently working for you and is moving in the right direction.

There are many acronyms and jargon for setting out effective targets and how to achieve them. I learnt SMART years ago, so it's certainly not the most modern of terms, but they all generally do the same thing, and as far as I'm concerned, if it isn't broken, don't fix it! I encourage you to think of your goals in SMART terms. That means making your goals:

S – specific – well defined and not vague

M – measurable – with a clear way of assessing whether it has been achieved

A – achievable – there's nothing more deflating than setting unrealistic targets, but that doesn't mean they can't be challenging

R – relevant – possibly the most important for ADHDers: make all goals consistent with your long-term goals

T – time-bound – give yourself a reasonable but defined time frame in which to achieve your goal.

If your energy is working with SMART targets in mind, you'll feel far more purposeful and will find that you can achieve so much more.

Playing the Game

Play is one of the best ways to manage ADHD symptoms in children – and especially those with boundless energy. There's no reason this shouldn't also apply to adults, but it's less easy and perhaps comfortable for adults to duck out of the office for a quick game of skipping rope! The solution to this (rather unfair) societal double standard has become adult ADHD toys. Yes, the word toys is still allowed!

There are hundreds of toys available with several different functions and ADHD benefits, but they can be broken down into several categories. Below are details of the main and most recommended toys for ADHD under each category. Sites like eBay and Amazon have specific categories for them. They have become incredibly popular, so use this concentrated list to decide what might be helpful to you and then go wild! (Or should that be go less wild and more focused?!)

Fidget toys for ADHD
Fidget toys are meant to be fairly discreet and non-disruptive. They tend to be small toys that fit into your hand and allow you to play with buttons, switches, chains, and basically anything that moves, so that the need to be "doing something" is satisfied,

allowing your mind to concentrate better on whatever task is at hand.

Popular fidget toys for ADHD include:

- the Rizzle or Noah – a metal toy with joined rings which allows you to spin various rings around with your fingers;
- the tangle toy – a bendy loop which can be plied into whatever twists and shapes the user decides;
- the Fidget Cube – a cube with different movement mechanisms on each face, including switches, buttons, dials, and more;
- pen/pencil fidget toppers with screw and nut mechanisms;
- beaded bracelets like Buddhist prayer beads – they provide plenty to quietly entertain your fingers so that your mind can be elsewhere;
- stress balls – one of the original fidget toys, these aren't just useful for relieving stress, but can also improve mental focus;
- chewing toys – these often come as necklaces, but not necessarily; many ADHDers prefer to chew than fidget with their fingers, and of course, gum can also help if this is the case;
- Doodle Pads also work excellently to direct unwanted excess energy and aid concentration.

Calming toys for ADHD

Calming toys are designed to relax the mind and provide a break from the constant buzz of the ADHD mind and body. Good options here include the stress balls and putty, but also sensory water beads: little drops which, when soaked in water, become a tactile relaxation bucket of loveliness! Heated and essential-oil scented wheat pillows can also work wonders when it comes to relaxation. For children (or adults who aren't afraid to admit they're above them), these often come inside soft toys. "Worry beads" and similar items like the Buddhist prayer beads also double up as good as calming devices.

Organizational toys for ADHD

Less to do with distracting the energy, and more to do with helping to direct your energy towards your goals, organizational devices such as To-do-list notepads, key finders, smart watches and phones, liquid/sand timers, and fun alarms can all work to help you become more organized and productive with your energy.

Food for Thought

One of the most discussed aspects of ADHD relates to nutrition. There is much science to support that what we eat affects our behavior, and the studies in nutrition and ADHD are no exception. Scientific camps tend to be fairly polarized on the subject though, with some claiming there simply isn't enough evidence to support a connection between food and ADHD, while others go so far as to claim the link is undeniable.

Celebrity chef Jamie Oliver claims that his nutritional program helps him to manage his ADHD, and sites like www.mumsnet.com are very proactive in supporting the scientific research with numerous case studies of their own as well as blogs from parents who rave about their own success stories. Some scientists, such as Dr. Lidy Pelsser of the ADHD Research Center from the Netherlands, even claim that food causes ADHD. It's clearly a hugely important topic.

The nutritional advice for ADHDers is sound advice for everyone, but the facts largely support the notion that processed foods and foods with additives are a bad choice. But you knew that anyway, right? Most of us choose to ignore the health warnings surrounding these sorts of foods because we live lives of convenience and it's difficult to make time to shop and cook properly. My message to ADHDers is: make the time. The evidence is so strong that it's worth it.

Artificial coloring, preservatives, pesticides, sulfites, artificial flavoring, artificial sweeteners, monosodium glutamate (MSG), sugar, and caffeine have all been closely linked with exacerbating – or even causing – the more negative and frustrating ADHD symptoms.

Conversely, Omega-3 fatty acids are believed to help improve brain function; consequently, a diet containing Omega-3 rich foods is recommended for ADHDers. Anything that helps the brain to work better is a good thing. Foods with high Omega-3 content are fish such as tuna, salmon, and other coldwater fish, and various seeds and seed oils. Flaxseed oil is a particularly good source.

Whichever scientific camp you believe in, there's certainly nothing to be lost by cutting down on processed foods and eating a diet naturally rich in vitamins and nutrients. Happy body, happy mind!

Mastering your energy through the use of mindful techniques, complementary therapies, ADHD toys, and nutrition is just one way of accelerating your journey towards ADHD confidence and self-acceptance. Once you are using your energy to actively achieve specific goals, the game is much easier to win. I hope some of the ideas in this chapter will point you in the right direction and help you turn your "raw, untamed, wild rumpus energy" to your advantage.

8 IN THE DRIVING SEAT

An ADHDer's energy, hyperfocus, and passion typically add up to one thing: ambition. This is especially true once an ADHDer begins to recognize how to make their ADHD symptoms work for them, which hopefully you're well on the way to realizing by now.

Once you are working in synergy with your ADHD, there's so much you are capable of achieving. And ambition is spurred by the one thing an ADHDer never lacks: drive. Have you ever found yourself so completely stubborn and determined to achieve a particular goal (whether it was a math problem in school, fixing the car, or writing a work report) that you became not only hyperfocused and engrossed in the task, but you stuck at it for hours on end – hours, days, weeks after others would have admitted defeat – until you finally achieved the outcome you were seeking? This is a common reality for most ADHDers.

This predisposition to relentlessly forge towards an end goal is part of your ADHD make-up, and is partially responsible for the reputation you're likely to have of being someone who gets stuff done and achieves the impossible. I love the saying: "Those who say it can't be done should stop interrupting the person doing it." It sounds like it could have been said by Kamprad or Neeleman, doesn't it?

Full Speed Ahead

As with most things we've talked about, there are

some potential pitfalls to have such a single-minded, focus on any particular goal. Motoring on at full speed will get you to your destination more quickly, but it also means there will be things you miss along the way, like the scenery, the joy of travelling with your family (once the "are we there yet"s have dried up, that is!), and most importantly, you'll risk missing the driving experience, which is where we gain all our learning and experience.

It also implies that you are always stuck being the one in control (which is typical and preferred ADHD behavior), but this means you can't share and brainstorm ideas with others having the shared experience. And there's important learning to be gained from this. We'll come back to the idea of control later in this chapter.

The analogy goes further; if you're headstrong and pursuant on a one-way road mission, you have the potential to ignore the other possible routes available to arrive at the same goal. We've learnt that ADHDers are great lateral thinkers and can come up with many different ideas to solve a problem. Be sure to give yourself a chance at this by letting the pressure off the pedal once in a while.

It's also much easier to react to potential obstacles in the road (these could be changes in your medication, your reaction to a medication, curve balls thrown by colleagues and superiors at work, a health crisis, etc.) if you're capable of slowing down every now and then, stepping back (using some of the techniques we looked at in chapter four), and assessing the bigger picture.

Nurture your drive and ambition – they are commodities that set you apart from the rest; ADHD is a common recurring factor in inventors, explorers, and discoverers. Just be willing to pop your head up from the wheel every now and then so that you can appraise your progress and re-evaluate the best route ahead.

Stick Shift vs Automatic

An ADHDer likes to be in control. I hesitate to use the term "control freak" because of the negative connotations it harbors, but I'm sure you understand what I mean. Wanting to be completely in charge of something can be beneficial because it means you are always in full possession of all the information all the time, but it does become rather burdensome.

Delegating tasks and managing your staff and time more efficiently will often lead to a spurt in productivity, which brings you that much closer to your goal. If you're tired while driving, you're supposed to stop, so it's ok to give someone else a turn at the wheel as long as you're still in the car.

I took a holiday with my husband in the UK several years ago, before we had the kids. It was great, beautiful even, but we nearly didn't get to see anything of the country at all. It turns out most cars in the UK are stick-controlled, and as we hadn't specifically requested an automatic with the hire car company, they were unable to help us out by swapping the car when we got there.

After we both got over our panic (neither of us is used to the driving stick) and bunny-hopped the car out of the parking lot, we got used to the concept quite quickly. We then realized just how much more control a stick shift gives you on the road. We're both lazy drivers, and I'm not sure we've ever driven a stick since, but having to consciously think about the process of driving again opened our eyes to every aspect of our driving ability, and we became much more conscious drivers while we toured the UK (especially in central London, where the traffic is complete chaos!).

My point is this: being fully conscious of both how you are driving towards your goals and the route you are taking makes you a better driver all-around. Use your ADHD determination and drive to ensure you're going to get there in the end, however many roundabouts you have to maneuver round (the UK seems to be obsessed with them!).

I fully appreciate that it can be difficult for an ADHDer to find this kind of drive when dealing with tasks and responsibilities which don't fully engage them. Try to use your creativity to turn these tasks into things you can enjoy. Perhaps set yourself timed challenges and targets with rewards for success, or find ways of building the things you love into the activities you don't.

Olympian Michael Phelps' mom did this with his schooling. He hated math but loved swimming, so she tried to combine the two in order to engage him with his homework: meters per second swum, water depth and volume of a swimming pool, etc. It isn't just wrapping the problem in pretty paper; it's making the less manageable more manageable.

Apply your drive and ambition in this way to making the most of your ADHD, and the journey becomes so much more pleasurable.

9 CONFIDENCE AND COMPETENCE

Herein lies one of the dichotomies of ADHD. While some ADHDers find themselves depressed and full of self-loathing, many others are prone to feeling incredibly confident most of the time – sometimes even over-confident.

This chapter is all about helping you find the right balance of confidence so that you feel able to achieve your goals without feeling overwhelmed or being overbearing. Take my ex-colleague. He was a very capable man in the world of finance, but was so full of his own self-importance and ability to read the markets that he made few friends in the business and ultimately had no portfolio to manage. He was perfectly competent but over-confident.

In contrast, there were plenty of confident newbies coming on and off the floor who lacked the competence to succeed (that is, until they had put in the time and practice required to learn the skills). Ideally, you need the perfect balance of both.

The good news for ADHDers is that they tend to be inherently competent in their chosen profession or endeavor because they are unlikely to be pursuing a path that doesn't interest them. Consequently, every ADHD advantage comes into play, and they will work hard at becoming competent very quickly.

For those ADHDers who are coming from a place of low self-esteem, confidence can seem a long way off, but you'll be surprised how quickly a person can become confident once they've been diagnosed and are managing their ADHD to their advantage. As I mentioned before, the turnaround in my neighbor's son was incredible, and there's no reason other ADHDers can't make the same sort of progress incredibly quickly.

Then there are the ADHDers who have spent so long as the center of attention, wowing the crowd with their vivacious personality, that they have become overconfident. They eventually lose their "following," and consequently their confidence, and might end up in a cyclical downward spiral of extremes. There's a fine line between arrogance and confidence, and just because ADHD is undoubtedly a benefit, it does not make you superior.

Many ADHDers carry themselves with a natural confidence that forms part of their charm. The aim is to master this level of confidence and pair it with the competence you've achieved with your drive and ambition, visionary thinking, and persistence.

Contrary to popular belief, confidence is not something you are born with (or without), and neither is it determined by achievement. Like many of the other ADHD skills we've been developing in this book, confidence is something that can be grown, practiced, and nurtured. Of course, that also means it can be lost, but we'll look at ways of helping to maintain confidence levels even in the face of failure.

Our first task is to determine exactly what level of confidence you're starting with so that you can access the right advice. To that end, here's an old school magazine-style quiz that should be both a bit of fun as well as an eye-opener. I was a sucker for these when I was younger, but never, in truth, gave much merit to the results. Perhaps that's because I was always a pretty confident and self-assured teenager.

This quiz is based on a number of reputable sources as well as a healthy amount of common sense. In order to get the most accurate result, it's important you're honest with yourself – no one need know what answers you've given but you. If you're going to get the most out of this, you have to be faithful to what you know your personal response to be. Don't cheat the system just so you can pat yourself on the back and tell yourself you're already the perfect level of confident. Of course, it may well be that you answer honestly and indeed are the perfect level of confident – in which case, go you!

If you find yourself torn between two responses, ask yourself these questions: start with, "What was my most recent response to this sort of situation?" If you can't think of a similar situation having occurred recently, then ask yourself, "What would my most typical and frequent response be to this scenario?"

It's important to consider the most recent event first so that you are measuring your current level of confidence. It may well be that, given confidence levels fluctuate, you've reacted differently in the past to how you might act now, so try to answer on the basis of being in the current moment for the best advice. Of course, once you've acted on any advice, you can always take the quiz again and reassess yourself!

Self-Assessment

Q1. There's a promotion opportunity at work. Do you:

      a.   Strut into the boss' office and tell him

exactly what salary you'll be requiring for your supreme skills.

b. Draft your application, give it a quick scan through and email it straight to the boss. He already knows how good you are, so you'd expect an interview.

c. Draft and redraft an application. Check it through very carefully. Feel you deserve to be considered and that you'd do the job well.

d. Begin drafting an application, but talk yourself out of applying. If they'd wanted you, they'd have just promoted you rather than posting the position for anyone to apply for.

e. Don't even consider drafting an application. You've probably reached your limit and aren't even sure you do this job well enough.

Q2. You arrive at a party, and there's no one you know there yet. Do you:

a. Move your way to the center of the dancefloor and prepare to change the world for the fans who've yet to meet you.

b. Head for the bar and order a drink for yourself and the cute redhead who looks like she/he is on her/his own too.

c. Greet the host, introduce yourself to the others he/she may be talking to, and go from there.

d. Stand awkwardly at the edge of the room looking at your phone until someone you know arrives.

e. What party? No one likes me enough to invite me to a party…

Q3. You're standing in line, and someone from behind you pushes in front when the teller asks who's next. Do you:

a. Grab him by the back of his pants, haul him back and give him a lecture on social etiquette the whole store gets to hear.

b. Loudly exclaim that there are such things as queues and wouldn't it be nice if people understood that.

c. Tap him on the shoulder and politely explain that you were next in line and you'd like to take your turn accordingly.

d. Mutter frustratedly under your breath.

e. Assume he probably had a good reason, and turn to ask if anyone else behind you is in a desperate hurry and offer them your spot. You can come back later.

Q4. You're asked to take part in a group project at work. Do you:

a. Use this as your opportunity to finally demonstrate some of your incredible ideas by taking the lead and making sure only your ideas are used.

b. Get incredibly frustrated when your ideas aren't the ones voted for, and reassert your opinion, but more loudly this time.

c. Make useful suggestions, possibly taking the lead, while listening to others and collaborating to create an outcome which meets the objectives.

d. Offer one idea, but decide to keep quiet and refrain from further contributions when it doesn't get heard.

e. Volunteer to get everyone a cup of coffee while the brainstorm session is taking place. That's probably why you're on the team anyway.

Q5. After years of difficulty, your doctor diagnoses you with ADHD. Do you:

a. Question the diagnosis. You did your own google research, and you think you have something far more rare.

b. Shake your head and explain to the doctor that you couldn't possibly have ADHD because you don't behave badly.

c. Feel as though everything suddenly fits and go home to do your research with a vague inkling that you might be able to make this work for you now you know what's what.

d. Have a mild panic attack. Isn't ADHD something awful that means no one will employ you ever and you'll never be able to achieve anything?

e. Nod and accept your fate. You've never amounted to anything, and now, at least, you have a reason to explain why you never will.

Q6. How do you feel about life in general?
- a. I am bossing it. They'll rename the US after me before long.
- b. I am climbing the ladder of success. I'm pretty near the top already, and I do not doubt in my ability to reach it soon.
- c. I am happy with where I am in life but have some important goals I am keen to achieve.
- d. I wish I had achieved more, but I've always felt like something was holding me back.
- e. I feel like I'm taking up room.

Q7. How do you deal with challenges?
- a. I laugh in the face of challenge. Nothing stops me getting what I want.
- b. I try to smash through any obstacles, sometimes causing a little damage, but it means I get to where I need to be.
- c. I work out the best way to approach them and ask for help if needed, usually passing them having learnt from the experience.
- d. I'll give things a go, but if they prove slightly difficult, I'm likely to back away and rethink my path.
- e. I turn and run.

Q8. You see yourself in the bathroom mirror. Your first thought is:
- a. Rocking it as always!
- b. Looking good today.
- c. There I am! Smile!

   d. Ugh, look away quickly. No one, least of
       all me, wants to see that.
   e. Mirror? What mirror? I wouldn't want
       one of those within a kilometer of my
       house!

Results

It doesn't take a genius to work this out, but I'll
spell it out just in case you're not confident enough in
your assessment.

Mostly As: Your self-confidence is off the scale, to
the point where you're probably incredibly annoying
to those around you. I'd be surprised if anyone
reading this book actually landed in this category, but
anything's possible! Think about practicing a little
humility and considering the needs of others. The
section on aggression below will be worth a read, as
would the section on assertion.

Mostly Bs: You're pretty confident, but teetering on
the verge of over-confident. It wouldn't hurt to heed
some of the advice below. Focus your attention on
the sections that deal with aggression, assertion, and
maintaining confidence.

Mostly Cs: You've got the balance right. You're
self-assured without being bullish or boastful. Take a
look at the advice on how to maintain this useful and
impressive level of surety.

Mostly Ds: You're lacking in confidence, but feel
you're capable of more. There's a lot of guidance for
people in these categories below. Take a specific look
at the sections on passivity and assertion. It won't
take much to boost you up into the realms of the
self-assured.

Mostly Es: You seem to have lost any faith that

you're even capable of being confident. Take heart. The fact that you're reading a book on how amazing ADHDers are suggests you are at least hopeful you can feel better. There's much that can help you below. Look specifically at the sections on self-efficacy and passivity, then the assertion section.

Self-Reflection

Now that you have a sense of how confident you are (or aren't), it's important to reflect on the actions you can take to improve your confidence levels and maximize your potential. While the general advice below applies to all, whether they have ADHD or not, there are some specific pointers regarding how ADHDers might best respond to some of the techniques. Remember: whatever level of confidence you feel you have, there is always room for self-betterment. As an ADHDer, the pursuit of anything worthwhile can be an engrossing task, which boosts dopamine levels and gives you a great sense of achievement. We'll start with advice for the least confident among you and work our way up to those who perhaps have got a little carried away with their own effervescent personality!

Self-efficacy
Understanding of self-efficacy is a great way to begin to feel more confident in yourself. Rather than a straight synonym for confidence, self-efficacy is more specific. It is your belief in your own ability to achieve a particular task – however great or small. Being conscious of your self-efficacy and rewarding yourself for the tasks and goals you achieve can give

your confidence small boosts – and they all add up! People with high self-efficacy see difficult tasks as challenges rather than impossibilities (that word we're not supposed to believe in, remember!). The ideal level of self-efficacy is slightly higher than your actual ability, i.e., you believe you can achieve slightly more than you probably can, as this encourages you to push yourself and in fact, achieve more (thereby also boosting your confidence).

You can improve your self-efficacy and consequently your confidence in a number of ways. Firstly, you can do it through your own achievements. Rather than focusing on things you feel you have no chance of achieving, consider the things you do feel capable of. Set yourself reasonable time frames in which to achieve them, and be mindful of your belief in achieving this goal. Start with tasks around the home, like making a family meal or clearing the kitchen. It's not about a race against the clock; it's about being reasonable with your expectations, believing in your ability to see a task through, and rewarding yourself mentally for doing it. Level up to tasks like being able to get the kids ready for school on time (a feat of co-ordination for any parent and a multitasking act ADHDers can thrive at if they are invested in the outcome, which is, in this case, boosting your confidence in your own ability to achieve small goals). Every time you achieve a difficult task, you boost your self-efficacy, even if it takes you several attempts to do it. Of course, you can then continue to level up until you are testing your self-efficacy for a major presentation at work, or you can even apply it to the management of your ADHD.

Secondly, you can boost your self-efficacy by watching other people achieve difficult tasks. Again, it's all about focusing on the positive. Seeing someone else achieve something difficult can make you believe it's possible.

Thirdly, seek encouragement. If your family, colleague, or significant other is supporting you with tasks and cheering you on, then it improves your determination to get them done.

Finally, simply by consciously trying to believe in yourself more, you are more likely to succeed. Give yourself a chance and practice being your own cheerleader. It may feel uncomfortable to begin with, but the more you do it, the more normalized the personal pep talks become. Google some positive affirmations. Louise Hay and her team at Hay House are fantastic at this. Follow them on social media for daily affirmations that will make you feel good about all aspects of your life!

Being Passive

You may have heard the word "passive" used in a positive way before, but trust me, it's not something you want to be if you're determined to win the ADHD brain game. Be stubborn with yourself about this! When we talk about passivity and confidence, being passive generally means allowing others to take advantage of you, and often, to walk all over you, so that they reach their goals, and you're left trampled into the mud. Let's get one thing straight: it is perfectly possible to be a kind and generous person without being passive. Kindness and generosity do not begin with letting others abuse you or your position. It's true to say that if you've been a passive person for a long time, your self-confidence is likely to be incredibly low. You probably feel like people "use" you and that you're always the one left behind. As an ADHDer, you may well have employed being passive as a defense mechanism. It's easier to not take part than to be told off for being pushy, or to be ridiculed for daydreaming should the activity not spark your interest.

But passivity breeds a lack of confidence, so it needs to be eliminated from your lifestyle. It begins with finding your own voice and learning to speak up without fear of being wrong, ignored, or laughed at. As with just about everything else we've discussed, this can only happen with practice and some inevitable trial and error.

Begin with yourself. Talking out loud to yourself – in a mirror if you feel comfortable, but you can build up to that if not – and vocalizing your own set of values, beliefs, and goals is a great way to get used to the sound of your own voice and to trust what it says.

Move on to being more assertive with people you feel comfortable around – most likely friends and family – until you feel confident enough to assert yourself in front of superiors and strangers. Trusting your own voice and opinion takes time and experience. Use your ADHD skills of persistence and resilience to help with this. The next section on assertiveness will help you to understand how confidence is effectively presented and well-received. If you scored mostly Ds and Es in the quiz, be sure to read this section too.

Assertiveness

Being assertive is the ultimate expression of self-confidence. If you are assertive, you are neither passive nor aggressive, but instead, you are in complete control of your emotions, your objectives, and, as a consequence, the probable outcomes of any given situation.

Being assertive is about many things, but it begins with knowing what you want to achieve. It's the same principle for management in the workplace. You can't manage a productive, efficient, happy team if there is a lack of direction and consequent uncertainty.

Take the example in the quiz which relates to a brainstorming meeting with a newly established task force. In order to voice your opinion assertively, you first need to be confident about the group's objectives. Then you need to voice your opinion in turn with others, listening to their ideas and perhaps adapting your own accordingly as you go. Being assertive is mainly about stating your honest opinion, listening to others, responding in a calm, reasoned manner, and working towards a conflict-free solution. You can plausibly be resolute in your opinion, but you may have to agree to disagree with someone else – this is fine! Don't be afraid to have different opinions to others, but do be prepared to voice your own opinion and then potentially have to compromise. After all, you're all ultimately working towards the same goal.

My daughter is currently learning how to be assertive. It isn't natural for her at all – she's instinctively aggressive when presented with a situation she doesn't like. I think it comes from having an older brother and not being sure how to positively make her voice heard. This is something we're working on. Fortunately, her teachers are on the same page as me. Breaking assertiveness down to junior school level makes it pretty simple to understand, so here goes.

At the beginning of the school year, she spent what felt like hours picking out new school stationery in the store. She'd saved some birthday money in order to indulge her obsession with pencils, erasers, and basically anything pink and glittery that she could fit into her school pack. She was proud as punch going in with all her bits and pieces on the first day, ready to take on the world and learn. Once it came to story writing, she was distraught to find one of her favorite sparkly pens in the hand of her classmate. Instinctively, she snatched the pen back, and yelled at the girl that she "shouldn't steal things." The "thief" promptly burst into tears and was the one who received all the sympathy from the staff. Not a particularly unusual or satisfying situation for anyone!

The teachers and I have been working to explain to my daughter that aggression (yelling, snatching, or hurting other people's feelings) rarely ends in a happy outcome for everyone, or indeed anyone. Slowly, she is learning that the rules of being assertive instead of aggressive are far more likely to achieve a conflict-free resolution for all.

The rules are simple:
1. Say how you feel calmly but firmly, trying to remove any negative emotion from your voice and body language.
2. Listen to the viewpoint of the other person (your active listening skills will be useful here) and try to understand their perspective.

3. Maintain a calm, collected manner whilst expressing yourself as you both communicate with a mutual resolution in mind.

My daughter now gets that had she explained to her classmate that she was hoping to use that particular writing implement for her own story because she was fond of it, the classmate may well have simply handed her the pencil back and all upset would have been avoided. In fact, once this had been explained to my daughter, she even suggested that she might have offered an alternative pencil from her stash, which could have even sparked a more positive outcome and gained her a friend instead of an enemy.

Aggression
I'm not going to dwell on this section, as it's made fairly clear in the assertiveness advice above what aggression is, and I'm sure we all have a fairly clear understanding. However, aggression doesn't necessarily mean physical violence. It can be something as small as a snappy tone in your voice, or hostile gesticulating – pointing urgently or accusingly at someone is a great example. It provokes aggression in response and feeds antagonistic and defensive behavior, neither of which are conductive to productivity, resolution, or building confidence.

Maintaining Confidence
Being able to maintain confidence comes with lots of practice – my favorite thing, isn't it! But once you start noting the small things that you realize you've succeeded in, you need to keep doing that! Expect

slip-ups and expect things to knock you back every now and then, but that doesn't take away from all the times you have achieved and succeeded at being assertive and confidently expressing yourself. Make lists of achievements if necessary. Be conscious of your self-efficacy and wary of both doubt and aggression.

As an ADHDer, you'll be conscious that you're capable of whatever you set your mind to. And your ADHD can help you to become confident if you aren't already. If you are one of the lucky ADHDers who already have confidence nailed in the right measure, then be resolute with maintaining it at the right level and be generous with your advice to others. Confidence and competence so often go hand in hand with ADHD – don't be afraid to work at it a little if you need to.

10 LOVE ME, LOVE MY ADHD

One of the most joyous advantages of having ADHD is the charisma associated with being a confident ADHDer. The combination of that confidence with your extraordinary levels of energy and fascinatingly different approach to life can make for a heady mix of magnetic attraction!

In my opinion, few celebrity ADHDers exude this more than Ty Pennington. His enthusiasm for life, his whirlwind energy, and his empathic ability make his seemingly indefatigable ecstasy contagious. Don't get me wrong; I'm a happily married woman, but the man has some serious mojo going on!

I can honestly say the same for my ADHD friends who've conquered their mindset. One friend, a fellow writer, visibly lights up the room when he enters. People are drawn to him before he even speaks. And when he does, the passion with which he articulates his knowledge and experiences is part of what makes him such an extraordinary storyteller and successful author.

But it wasn't always that way – for either my friend or Pennington. Their diagnosis was the beginning of a journey of self-discovery and education, during which time both ADHDers learned to play to their strengths. Pennington's mom recognizes the irony of the situation (and consequently the significance of diagnosis and education). She says, "The very traits that once held Ty back are now his greatest assets." Certainly, his energy and quirkiness on camera are what makes him fascinating to watch. You want to be around him because you feel his infectious vibrancy, and there's no reason this can't be true for most ADHDers.

This magnetic charisma is the product of a number of ADHD gifts; most apparently: vitality, curiosity, and an ADHDer's capacity to love ferociously.

Vitality is a hugely attractive quality because those with a zest and enthusiasm for life naturally seem to be getting the most out of it. Those who lack this quality or feel they'd like to enrich their own vitality seek to do so by spending time with others who seem to have found "the secret." Of course, there is no "secret" as such, but those people in the world who revel in any sort of experience, exude positivity and demonstrate a thirst for living are exciting people to be around. They have stories to tell, ideas to share, and questions to ask. Well-educated and symptom-managed ADHDers are inclined to become these sorts of people because of their energy, confidence, creativity, and propensity for risk-taking. They are fundamentally interesting people to know and to be around.

The thing about curious people is that they become knowledgeable very quickly, and knowledgeable people are fascinating. An ADHDer's curiosity comes from their appetite to get as much out of the world as possible, which includes learning as much as possible and consequently promotes self-betterment. This makes them alluring because there's always something new to learn from them, even if it's a story about how they failed to achieve an aim and what they gained in the process. We are all curious on some level, but the most curious are attractive because they are always on the go; there's always something new happening in their lives and we long to be inspired or entertained by sharing in these experiences.

There's no denying that whatever an ADHDer decides to do, they do it fiercely, which can make them great romantic partners and lovers. Alongside their capacity to love deeply sits the ability to empathize deeply; consequently, people with ADHD are known for being incredibly compassionate. With an ADHDer as your friend, you are likely to feel understood. As an ADHDer, this comes with benefits and drawbacks. Yes, the world wants to be your friend, but boy can that be draining at times! Especially if they are all relying on you for their emotional needs. So as an ADHDer, that can be tough, and is something you should be conscious of. It's great to be in demand, and it works as a confidence booster, but remember to look out for your own emotional needs too. That might involve keeping some of your fans at a distance, or it might mean dipping into the self-pampering pool of ideas back in the "Burnout" section of chapter two.

Relationships can be a roller coaster with or without ADHD added into the mix. And, frustratingly, it's inevitable that with ADHD as an extra wheel in a romantic relationship things will get a little rockier than normal. The good news is that, with all parties working together to understand how ADHD might be affecting a relationship, everyone ends up better off. Remembering that communication is key from the outset, let's take a quick ride on that roller coaster and consider some of the potential highs and lows as well as how both partners can work towards evening out the track (without eliminating those great highs!).

Riding the Relationship Roller coaster

The statistics here are ugly. They seem to prophesize doom, so let's get the worst one over with quickly: marriages involving an ADHD partner are twice as likely to end in divorce. There. About as easy as ripping off a band aid, right? It's a hard pill to swallow, but there are plenty of people out there trying to redress the balance and reduce the statistic.

One of the most prominent experts on ADHD and relationships is Melissa Orlov. Her book *The ADHD Effect on Marriage* is based on her personal experience of marriage with an ADHDer and their own journey at overcoming the struggles. If you're after more detailed reading on this aspect of being an ADHDer, or if you're in a relationship with an ADHDer, (whether you think the relationship is struggling or not), then I'd absolutely suggest you give it a read.

There are quite a few articles readily available on the internet about this too. What appears here in this guide is a synopsis of the conclusions drawn from my own research. Use this as a starter to see if any of the common factors affecting ADHD relationships apply to your own, and consider the suggestions for how to improve each potential scenario.

The Dopamine Effect
It's well known that ADHDers run on lower levels of dopamine than non-ADHDers. Simply put,

dopamine helps to regulate the reward and pleasure centers in the brain. The thrill of a new relationship and the act of falling in love flood the system with dopamine – something an ADHDer isn't used to. Suddenly, the pleasure part of the brain is doing cartwheels and backflips while juggling glazed donuts dipped in chocolate. "What a rush!" the brain exclaims. "What incredible pleasure! This is amazing! I must have more of this…" Which can result in two things: either the ADHDer becomes a serial dater in order to experience this "high" more regularly, or the ADHDer becomes hyperfocused on his/her new relationship. Serial dating, we can probably recognize (once we've grown out of our twenties at least) as ultimately unfulfilling, but it can be a hard cycle to break. The key comes in recognizing the behavior pattern in order to break it. But as a non-ADHDer, having someone hyperfocused on you in a relationship sounds pretty cool, right? Wrong.

It may be amazing to start with, but once the dopamine effect wears off, you can be left with a partner who appears to have lost all interest in you – seemingly overnight. But it isn't that he/she has lost interest; it's just that the level of interest you received when they were hyperfocused is far above and beyond any normal level of interest. This sudden change in behavior is likely to leave the non-ADHD partner feeling neglected, unwanted, and potentially very sad.

Playing Parent

This is one of the most common issues between ADHD and non-ADHD partners. Typically, the non-ADHD partner ends up playing a "parent" role to their ADHD "child" counterpart. It's easy to fall into habits of clearing up after them, being responsible for the majority of the chores, trying to organize them and their calendar, suggesting how they could better achieve things, etc. This provides very little satisfaction for either partner. While "mothering" the ADHD partner might feel like a way of caring for them and showing them your support, it ultimately doesn't suggest an equally balanced relationship and can frustrate both partners immensely. Being in a happy relationship is not supposed to feel like raising a teenager! And how much do teenagers hate being treated like children rather than adults? Exactly. Falling into this pattern is going to end badly unless both partners can find ways to recognize the behavior and adapt themselves accordingly.

Nag, nag, nag

This can appear as an alternative to the parent-child dynamic above. Instead of the non-ADHD partner "mothering" their ADHD other half, they stand their ground and make demands that the ADHD partner do more around the house, change their behavior, and try harder. Essentially, what the non-ADHD partner is doing here is demanding that their other half stop being ADHD! It's as futile and ignorant as insisting someone with depression should "just lighten up," or someone with a stammer should "speak properly." Relationships that follow this path are very likely to end unhappily unless each partner plays their part in working towards a far more satisfactory and plausible solution than nagging.

So what measures can be put in place in order to

avoid these pitfalls and help to promote a happy, healthy, ADHD-inclusive relationship? The answer is "many." Below are a few pointers drawn from the research, which have been proven to restore harmony and contentment in relationships involving at least one ADHD partner.

Treatment and Education

Yup folks, it's at the top of the list again! It's vital that an ADHDer gets the right treatment (which can mean everything from meditation and mindfulness, through to toys and nutrition, to medication as we've already seen) in order to live the most successful (by which I mean happy) ADHD life possible. Naturally, this is going to apply to relationships too. By educating yourself about your personal version and level of ADHD, you arm yourself with the knowledge you need to access the best treatment program for yourself, and, equally as importantly, you are able to educate your partner about your specific ADHD manifestations and needs. Forewarned is indeed forearmed in this instance, and by communicating with your partner about what behaviors they might expect from you, you can help to prevent any potential disappointment. More than this, you can educate yourself and your partner in the most effective methods for responding to your particular ADHD behaviors. Which leads us on to the next strategy.

Communication

Communication is not a one-way street. Both partners need to be prepared to communicate how they are feeling, what they'd like to change/happen, and how best they think you should both approach the issue. Problems in relationships aren't always about ADHD behavior, and don't always require specialist solutions. They do, however, always require clear and honest (and calm) communication from both parties in order to work together towards a resolution. In the same way that both parties need to communicate and work towards resolutions, so it's important to understand that the problems you might experience aren't just a result of the presence of ADHD. While ADHD behaviors might be contributing to an issue, the response from the non-ADHD party is equally culpable for creating any particular given situation you and your partner might find yourselves in. There should be no blame game here. Understanding how you both could adapt behaviors and reactions is really important to appreciate.

Seeking Solutions (plural)

The point, of course, is that you are both on the same side and want to improve the relationship. Seeking ways of achieving this collaboratively is the best way to ensure you are successful in your joint endeavor. But it will inevitably require some trial and error. Not everyone can adapt their behavior instantly just because they are told it's causing friction. Things take time and effort. If you are both understanding during this process, then chances are you'll get to a better place.

It's important to remember that failure is OK. As long as you are both trying to find ways to make things better, then you're walking the same path hand in hand. Sometimes, one of you will trip up. That doesn't mean you can't pick each other up and carry on. For example, if the non-ADHD partner is finding it difficult to cope with the mess an ADHDer often creates, and feels like they always have to tidy up after them (very parent-child syndrome), simply explaining to the ADHDer that this is a problem isn't necessarily going to fix it. Look for creative ways towards a compromise. Perhaps see if there's one particular area you could focus on – the family room, for example. Leaving books and papers strewn across furniture and the floor means they're likely to get damaged by tiny feet or muddy paws; constantly doing the clear-up for the ADHD partner means it's likely they don't see this problem. Several creative solutions could be found here: the mess could be left to get damaged so that the ADHDer fully appreciates the issue and works to protect their things; the non-ADHD partner might clear them to an agreed area – the coffee table – and then it's up to the ADHDer to do the rest; you both might work on tidying the mess together, setting aside ten minutes to clear followed by ten minutes of snuggling on the now available couch as a reward. And, of course, there are many more options in between. The point is to find what works best for the two of you as a compromise – and remember, there is no blame here. If it doesn't get done, it doesn't get done. It's a learning and adapting process, not an ultimatum which will cause more friction and difficulty.

As we've already learned from Kamprad, failure is no bad thing. If one potential solution doesn't work, try another, and keep trying. Be patient and remember the long term goal: a happier, healthier relationship.

Schedule "us" time

I know, it doesn't sound sexy and spontaneous like the beginning of the relationship may have been, but it's sometimes necessary. If you know your ADHD partner is easily distracted by their other projects and is likely to forget an anniversary or a dinner date, remind them! You can't fix the ADHD (and why would you want to, given the good that can come from it too), so work with it instead. Similarly, if you know your ADHD makes you forget things or is causing your loved one to feel neglected, set reminders, plan things, and make time with each other a part of your weekly or daily schedule. Put it in the diary, or in your phone reminders alongside the mundane and the exciting, and keep to the plan.

Doing activities together is a great option for relationships involving ADHD. Walks, sports, and anything that means the ADHD brain is engaged in doing more than just one thing at a time also means they're more likely to be able to shower you with the attention you're craving.

This may sound like a frustrating solution, but trust me, even couples in relationships that don't involve ADHD benefit from scheduling in "us" time! Just try to make sure you're doing something that appeals to both of you on some level. My husband doesn't consider it valuable "us" time when I'm dragging him around the mall… and he has a point!

If you have kids, then there's an extra element to consider here. "Us" time is different to "family" time. Both are hugely important for long-term happiness in a relationship, so be careful not to substitute "us" time for "family" time. Build both into your regular schedule, and everyone will be better off for it.

When you're both working together to manage some of the more complicated aspects of an ADHD inclusive relationship, then it's easier to reap the rewards ADHD brings too. Who can't help but be proud that the brightest light in the room is their other half? You both get to benefit from the wide circle of friends and contacts. You're going to get far more party invites than most couples will! And then there's knowing that while one of you gets to boast about having the most charismatic of partners on their arm, the other gets to brag about having the kind of understanding and supportive significant other most people just dream about.

11 I CAME, I SAW, I CONQUERED

Accepting and nurturing the love of your significant other is one thing, but achieving self-love with ADHD is one of the ultimate goals that makes everything else so much easier. Of course, not that you're this far through the book, it's perfectly possible that you're oozing with the self-acceptance and self-love that I'm seeking to inspire!

But just in case it takes a little longer to see and believe, I want to do a little recap of the things you should be proud to own as part of your ADHD potential.

Visionary Thinking – seeing the world from a different perspective means that you have the ability to think up ideas and find solutions that others may not see. This can make you an incredible asset in the workplace.

Entrepreneurship – being able to take an idea from start-up through to completion is a valuable skill whether you're employed or working for yourself.

Detail-Oriented Eyes with a Big-Picture Perspective – the capacity to notice the little things, while at the same time being able to apply the significance of those details to the wider scheme of things, is a rare talent. Use it wisely, and you'll gain a reputation as someone who can do a job properly.

Creativity – with creativity bursting from your pores, you open up opportunities in both your working life and your personal life. Plus, this talent can come with the bonus of adding both therapy and fun to your busy world.

Risk Tolerance and Resilience – being unafraid to take risks, as well as being able to bounce back from adversity unscathed and undefeated, gives you a huge advantage over those who are too fearful to push the boundaries.

Energy – too commonly perceived as an ADHDer's downfall, the amount of energy you have makes you able to achieve the work of a non-ADHDer in less time. Properly harnessed and channeled, your energy makes you indefatigable, meaning you can conquer the world before breakfast and still be willing to take on the heavens before lunch.

Ambition and Drive – an ADHDer doesn't just "think big," but thinks bigger still. A non-believer in the word "impossible," you can achieve things others wouldn't bother attempting and prove that barriers are meant to be smashed through on the way to success.

Loving and Lovable – an ADHDer's capacity to love is immense, and only paralleled by the amount of love they receive in return. Use your charm with humility and purpose, and you'll be the ringmaster of this whole circus in no time at all.

With these attributes at your command, the world is yours to conquer. First, you must conquer your own mindset and truly believe that these characteristics are part of what makes you, you. In order to do this, you need to let go of the "lost years" – the time before you knew why you behaved the way you did and couldn't manage it properly – and embrace the future as the colorful kaleidoscope it promises to be after you've honed your skills in these areas and re-carved your path to success and happiness.

Use the above traits as column headings if necessary, and make lists under each about how you've already demonstrated these assets in your life to date. Once you've completed that list, add to it a set of goals you can use these proficiencies to help you achieve. Then go out and make it happen.

With the statistics suggesting that depression and self-loathing are more likely to be found in ADHDers than self-love, I challenge you to become a future ADHD champion: someone like Neeleman, who celebrates the positives of an ADHD diagnosis, rather than someone who buys into the negativity and allows themselves to feel victimized by the association. Because really, there is so much to embrace once you are managing your ADHD effectively.

My ADHD writer friend is slowly conquering his own world, publishing book after book and discovering more and more about different cultures and people – such is his drive and passion. Get him talking about ADHD, and he'll spiel for hours about the wonders of medication, hyperfocus, energy, and desire. And you'll be drawn into every word he utters because of his electric personality and enthusiasm. Be like him. Be one of the winners in the ADHD brain game. Love the person your ADHD makes you.

And, finally, learning to love your ADHD and recognizing the strengths associated with it is just the first step. I hope some of the exercises and ideas in this guide will be helpful to you and will encourage you to explore your potential fully. You've got nothing to lose!

One of my favorite sayings is: "Shoot for the moon; even if you miss, you'll land among the stars." With the right dialogue surrounding ADHD and the tools to make it work to your advantage, ADHD really can send you soaring. And the sky is not the limit. There is no limit. ADHD can empower you to achieve what you may previously have believed to be impossible. Embrace your gift, master your ADHD brain, and win the game. No tickets, dice, or cards required.

REFERENCES

This is by no means an exhaustive list, but it includes many of the websites, books and, studies I found most useful to my own research. Use this as a starting point and remember that your version (or your child's version) of ADHD is not a carbon copy of anyone else's. Listen to the research, but forge your own path based on your own knowledge of yourself and what is most likely to help you harness your ADHD advantage.

Positive Approaches to ADHD

https://www.additudemag.com/
http://www.webmd.com/add-adhd/guide/positives#1
http://www.healthline.com/health/adhd/benefits-of-adhd
http://adhdmanagement.com/

General Research

http://www.psychiatrictimes.com/adhd/diagnosis-and-management-adhd-adults

Michele Toner, Thomas O'Donoghue and Stephen Houghton, "Living in Chaos and Striving for Control: How adults with Attention Deficit Hyperactivity Disorder deal with their disorder", *International Journal of Disability, Development and Education* Vol. 53, No. 2, June 2006, pp. 247–261

Case Studies

http://www.kidsbehaviour.co.uk/adhd-case-study.html

http://www.medscape.org/viewarticle/513743_9

https://genesight.com/genesight-adhd-case-study-reducing-cycle-frustration-15-year-old-attention-deficit-hyperactivity-disorder/

http://www.kidsmatters.com.au/case-studies/

ADHD and the Entrepreneur

https://www.forbes.com/sites/dalearcher/2014/05/14/adhd-the-entrepreneurs-superpower/#4e8d783b59e9

http://www.coachingforadhd.com/adhd-blog/adults/the-adhd-entrepreneurial-brain-style/

http://www.coachingforadhd.com/wp-content/uploads/2013/12/UnlocktheSecretsEBS2015.pdf

ADHD and Hyperfocus

https://www.verywell.com/hyperfocus-and-add-20464

http://www.wisegeek.com/what-is-hyperfocus.htm#didyouknowout

ADHD and Complementary Therapies

https://aadduk.org/symptoms-diagnosis-treatment/complementary-therapies/

https://www.newhealthadvisor.com/Essential-Oils-for-ADHD.html

https://www.brainbalancecenters.com/blog/201
4/10/essential-oils-adhd

ADHD and Nutrition

http://health.howstuffworks.com/mental-
health/adhd/for-64-percent-of-kids-with-adhd-food-
is-the-cause.htm
http://www.webmd.com/add-adhd/guide/adhd-
diets#1
http://www.health.harvard.edu/newsletter_article
/Diet-and-attention-deficit-hyperactivity-disorder
http://www.healthline.com/health/adhd/foods-
to-avoid

ADHD and Exercise

http://www.everydayhealth.com/add-adhd/can-
you-exercise-away-adhd-symptoms.aspx
http://www.webmd.com/add-adhd/guide/adult-
adhd-and-exercise
https://www.theatlantic.com/health/archive/201
4/09/exercise-seems-to-be-beneficial-to-
children/380844/

ADHD and Mindfulness/Meditation

https://www.additudemag.com/mindfulness-
meditation-for-adhd/
http://www.huffingtonpost.com/alvaro-
fernandez/study-meditation-against_b_103534.html
https://sharpbrains.com/blog/2013/12/10/study
-does-mindfulness-meditation-training-help-adults-
with-adhd/

ADHD and Coaching

http://adhdmanagement.com/5-reasons-adhd-coaching-doesnt-work/

https://psychcentral.com/lib/what-is-adhd-coaching/

http://untappedbrilliance.com/adhd-coach/

ADHD and Toys

http://www.health.com/health/gallery/0,,20442916,00.html

https://www.focusfied.com/fidget-toys-help-adhd-add/

http://www.parents.com/health/add-adhd/best-toys-for-adhd/

ADHD and Medication

https://www.helpguide.org/articles/add-adhd/medication-for-attention-deficit-disorder-adhd.htm

http://www.healthline.com/health/adhd/medication-list

http://www.everydayhealth.com/adhd/guide/treatment/

ADHD and Relationships

Orlov, Melissa The ADHD Effect on Marriage: Understand and Rebuild Your Relationship in Six Steps (2010) Speciality Press / A.D.D. Warehouse

https://www.adhdmarriage.com/

ADHD and Creativity

https://www.psychologytoday.com/blog/here-there-and-everywhere/201106/is-the-adhd-brain-more-creative

http://www.inquisitr.com/1599794/adhd-and-creativity-new-research-says-adhd-is-being-mistreated-in-schools/

http://thecreativemind.net/825/adhd-creative-min

26461385R00067

Printed in Poland
by Amazon Fulfillment
Poland Sp. z o.o., Wrocław